I0499845

This book belongs to

....

....

....

....

....

....

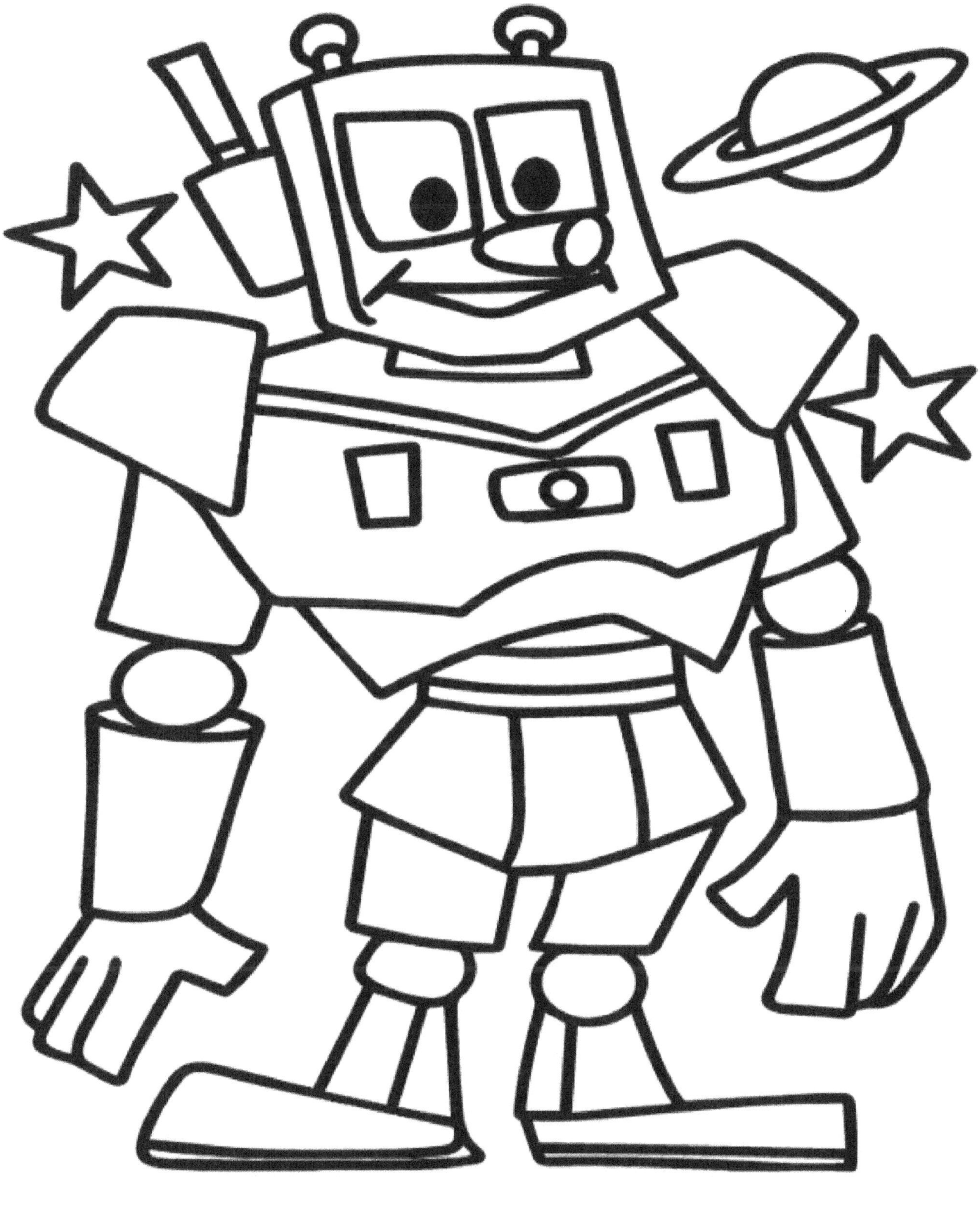

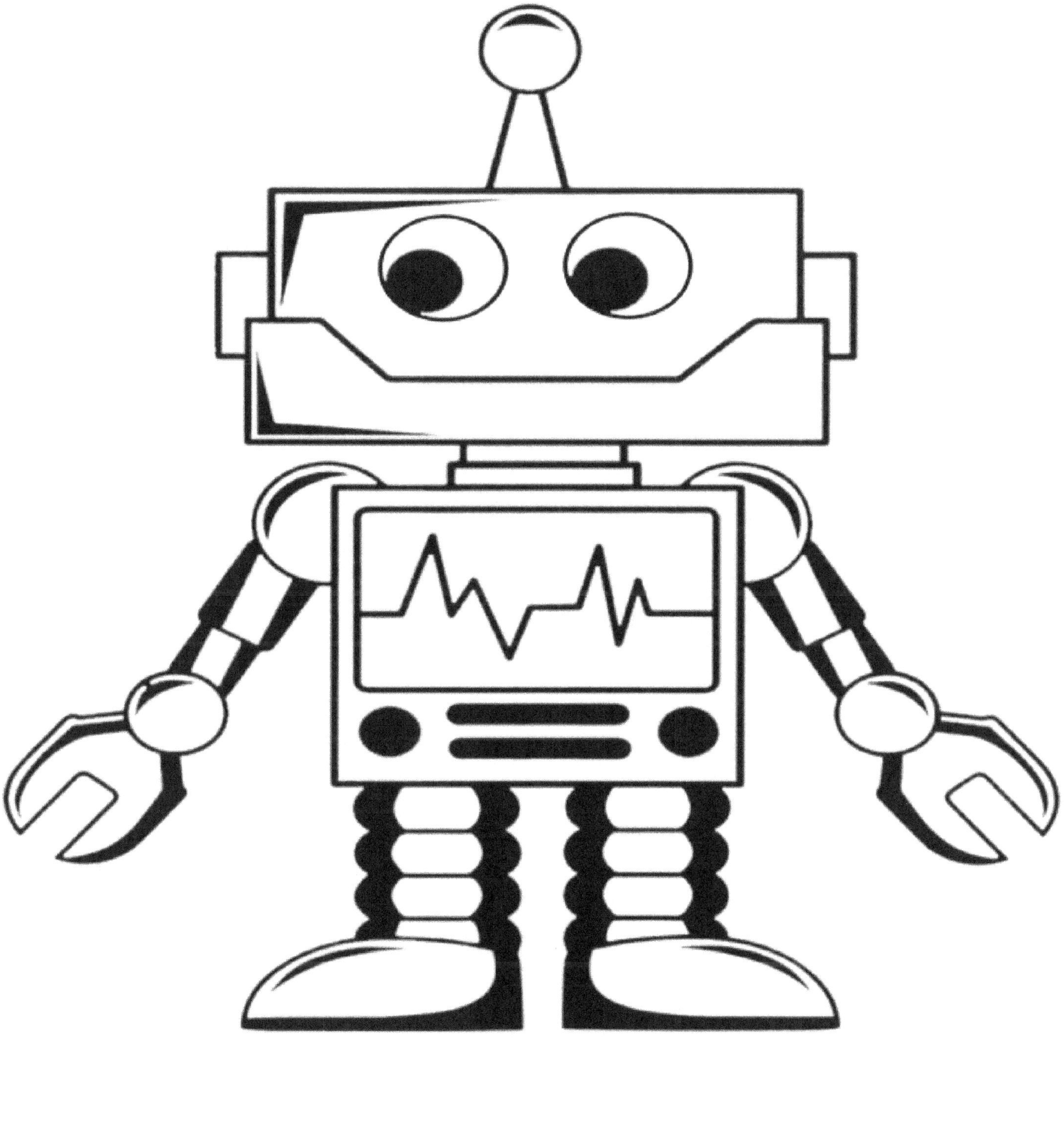

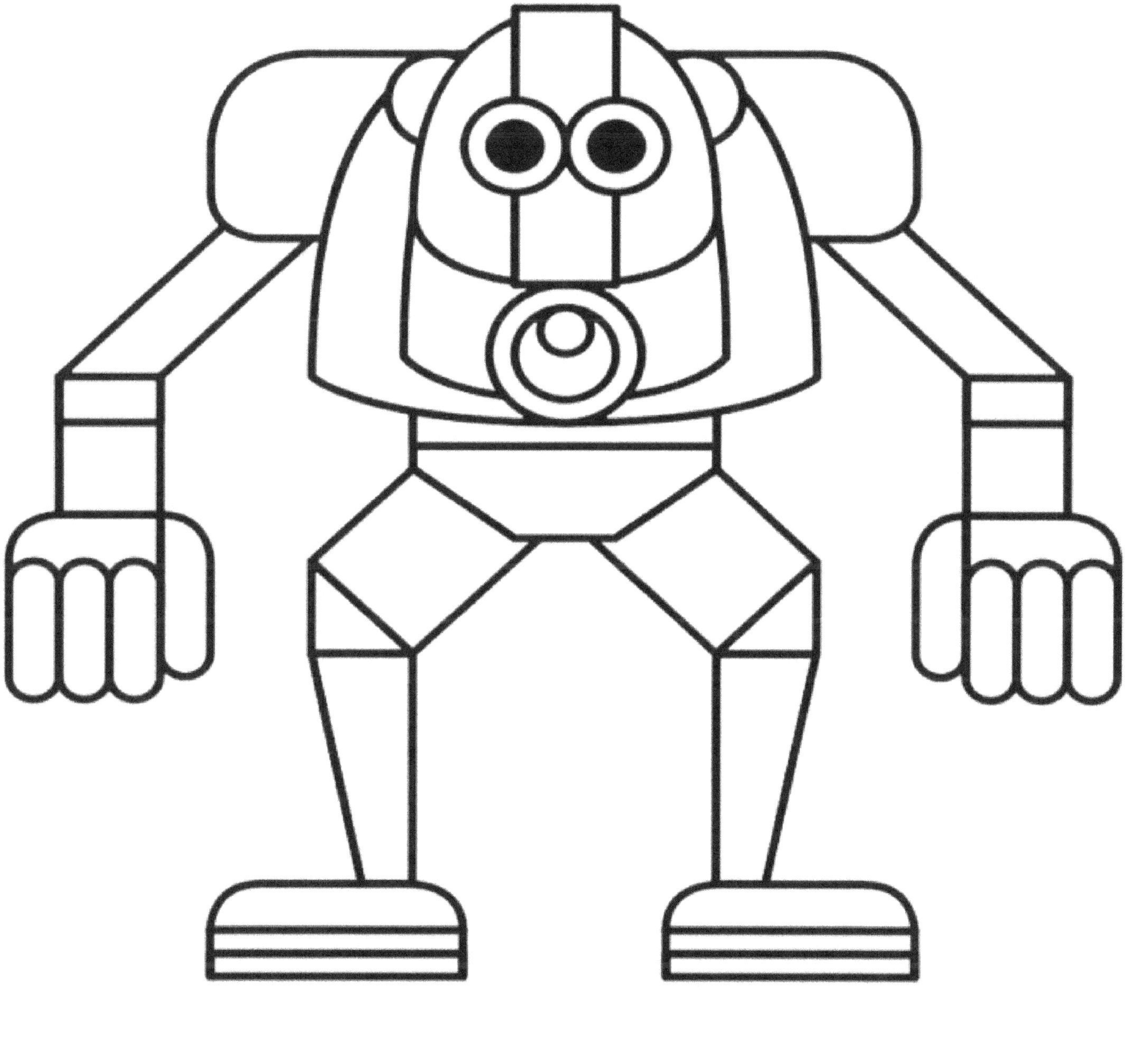

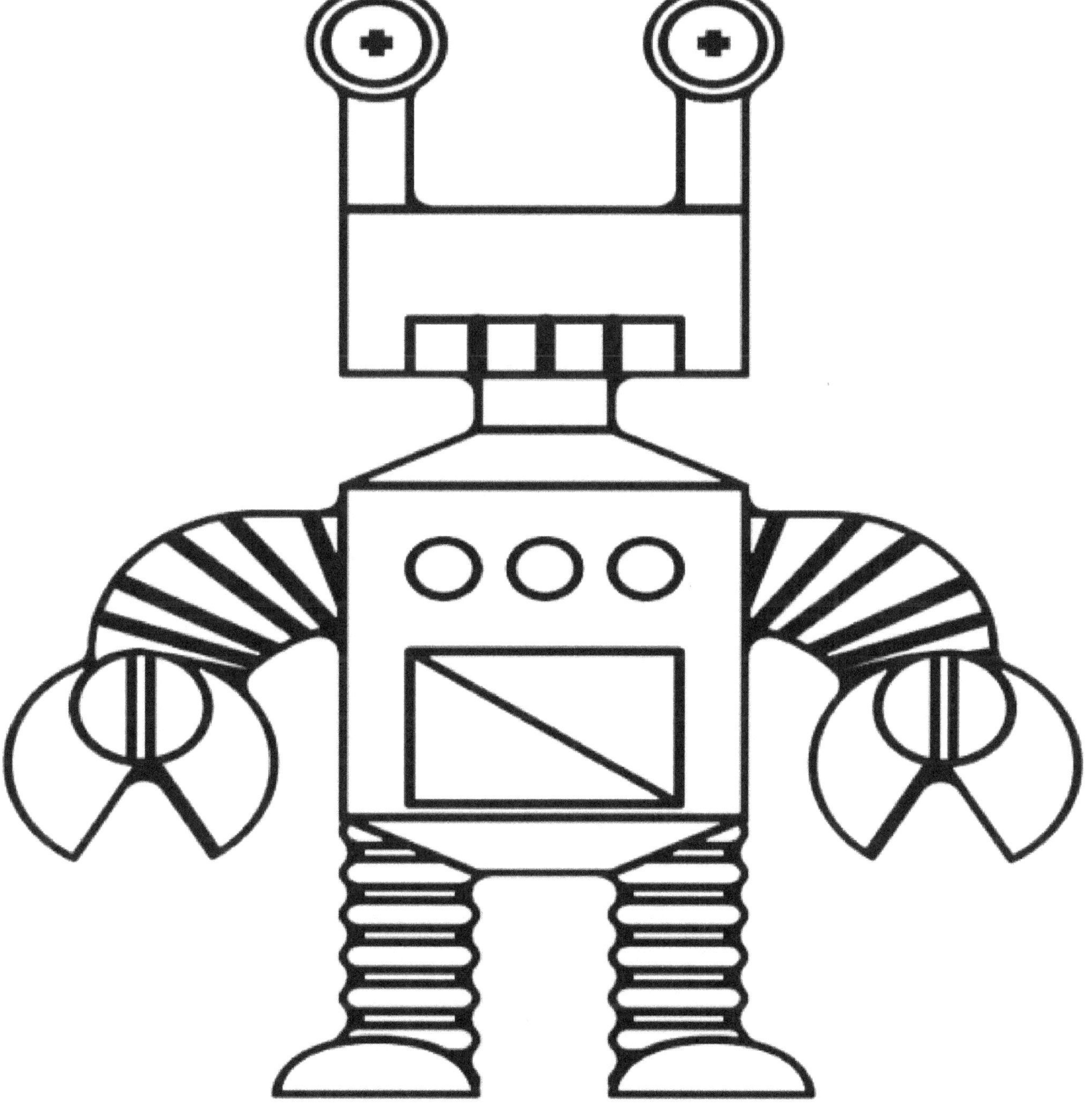

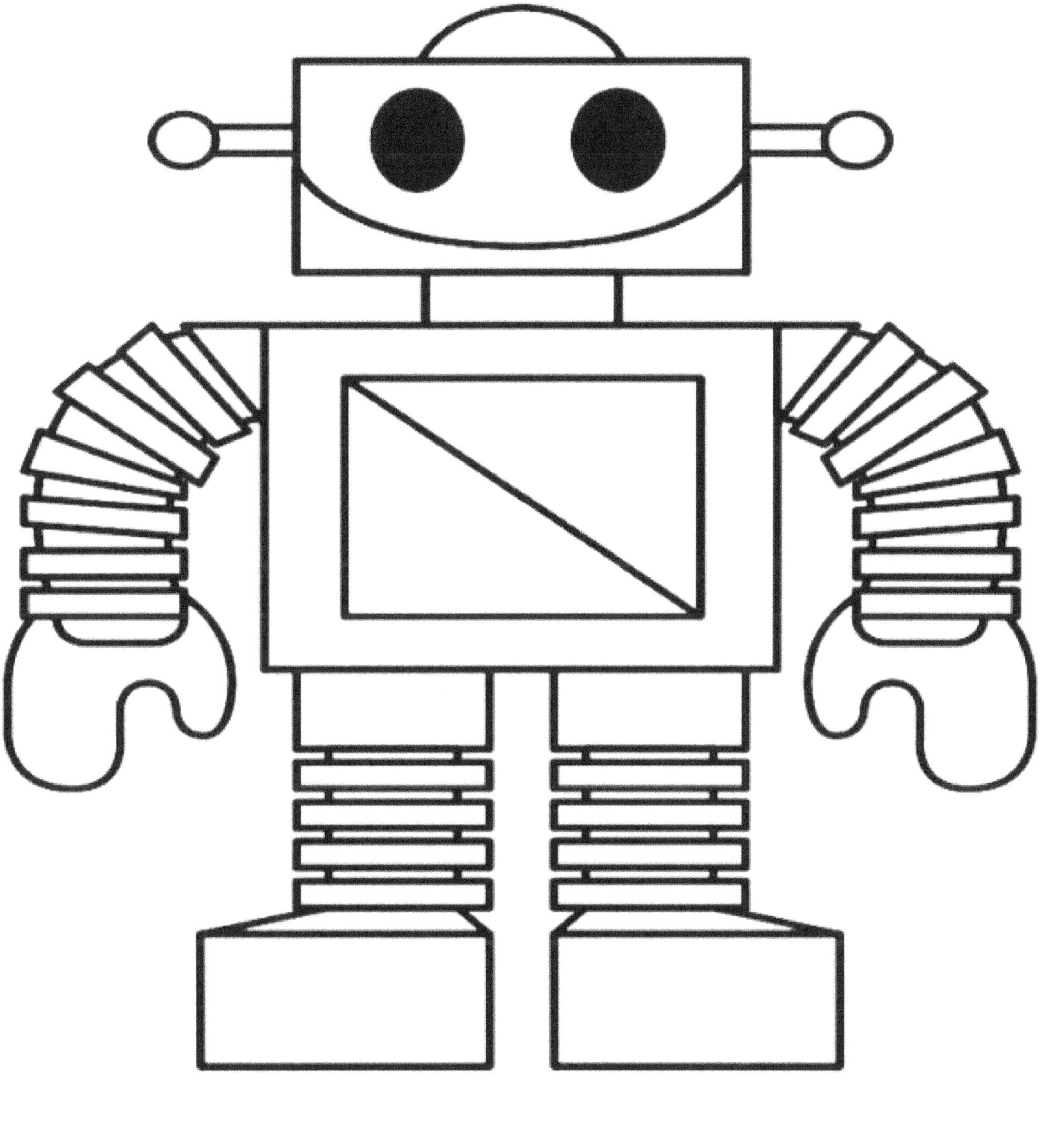

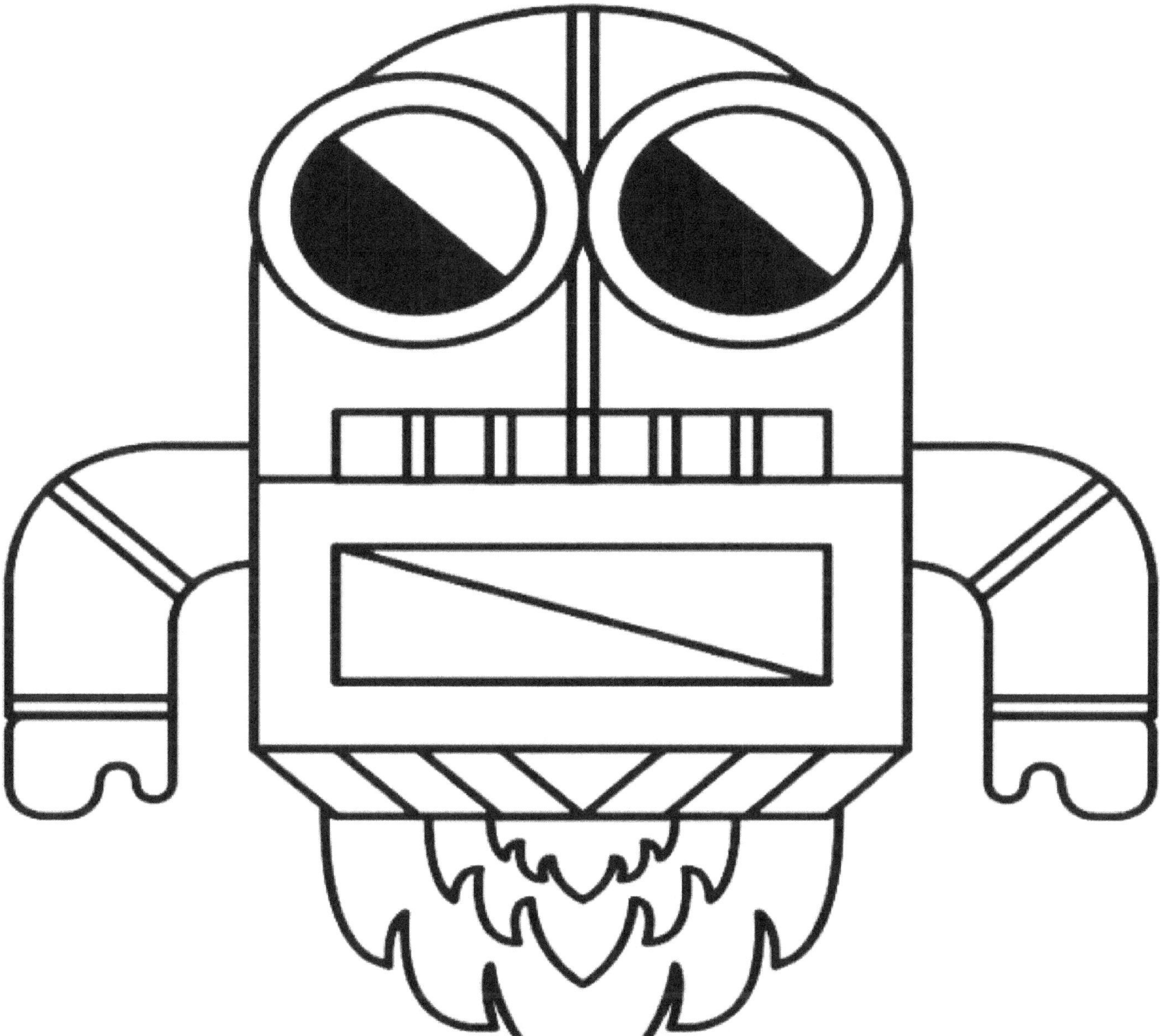

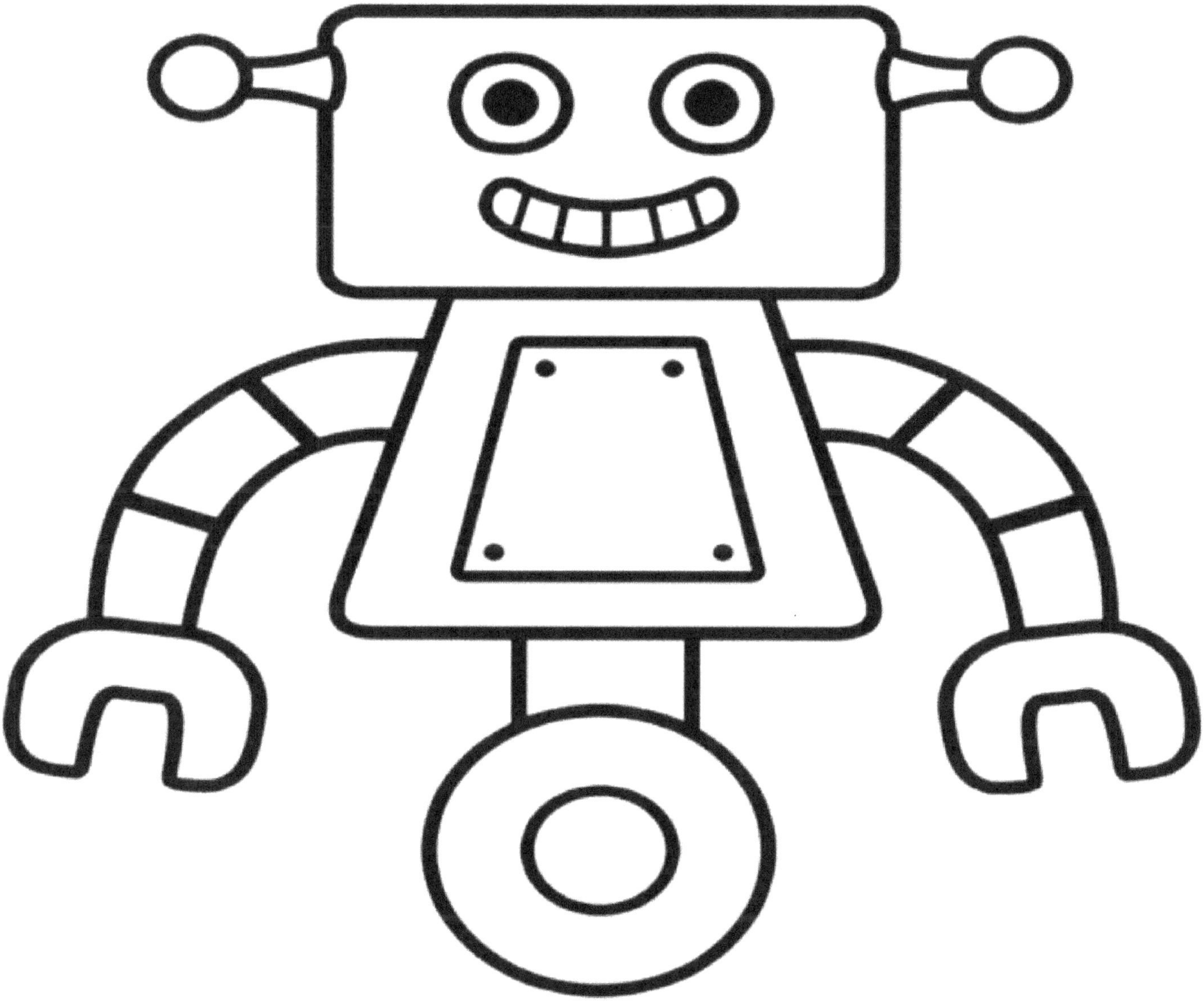

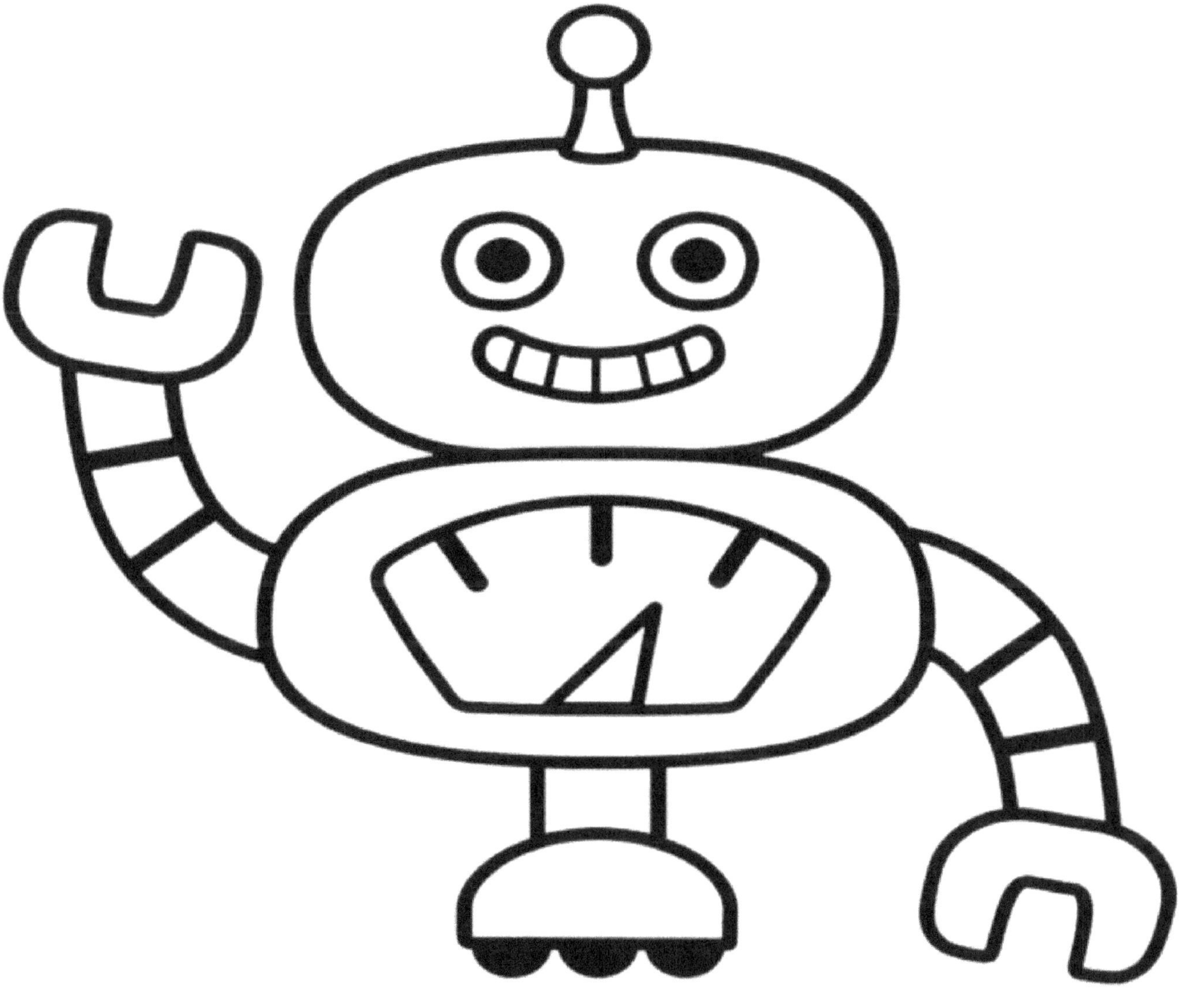

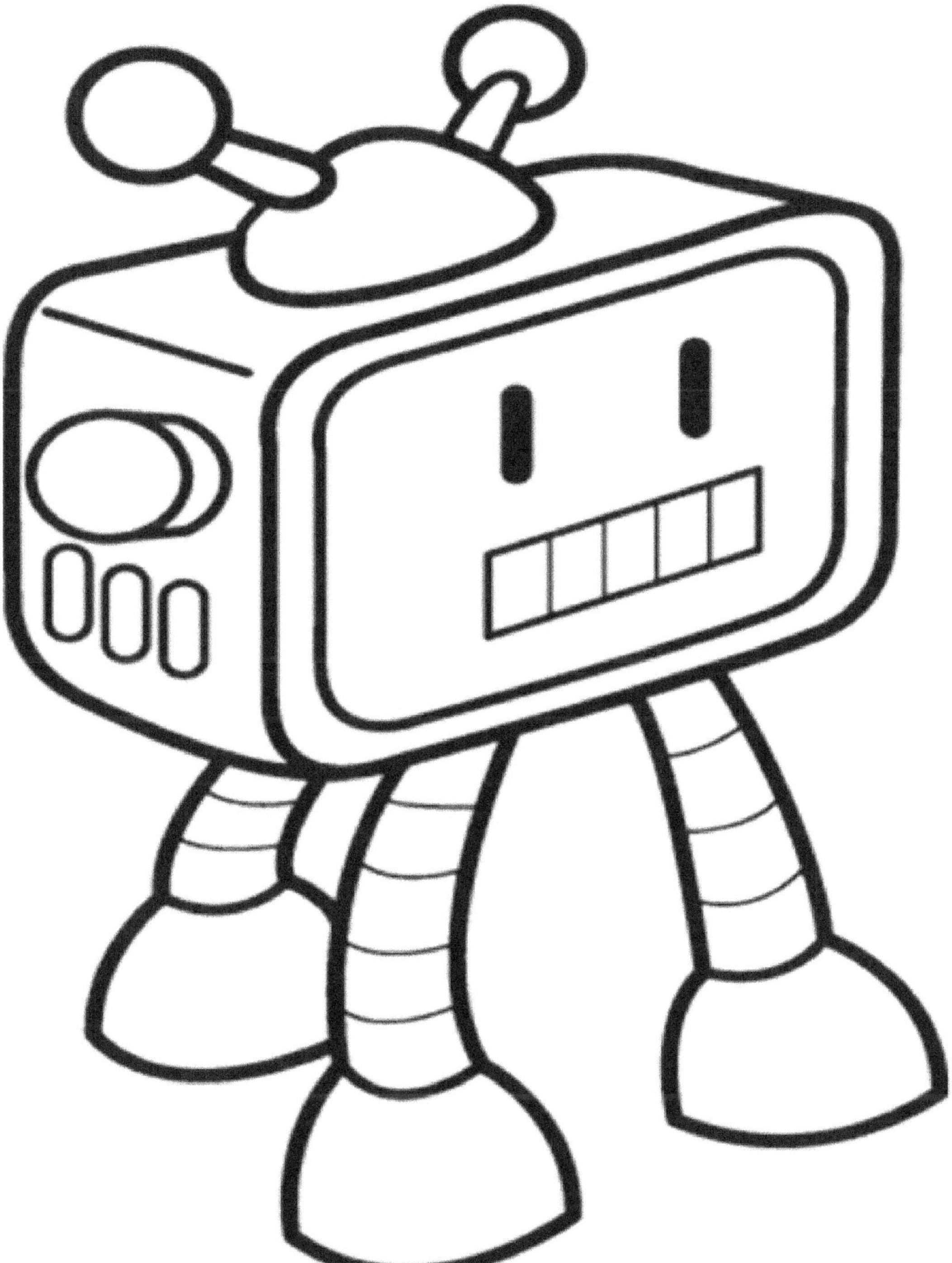

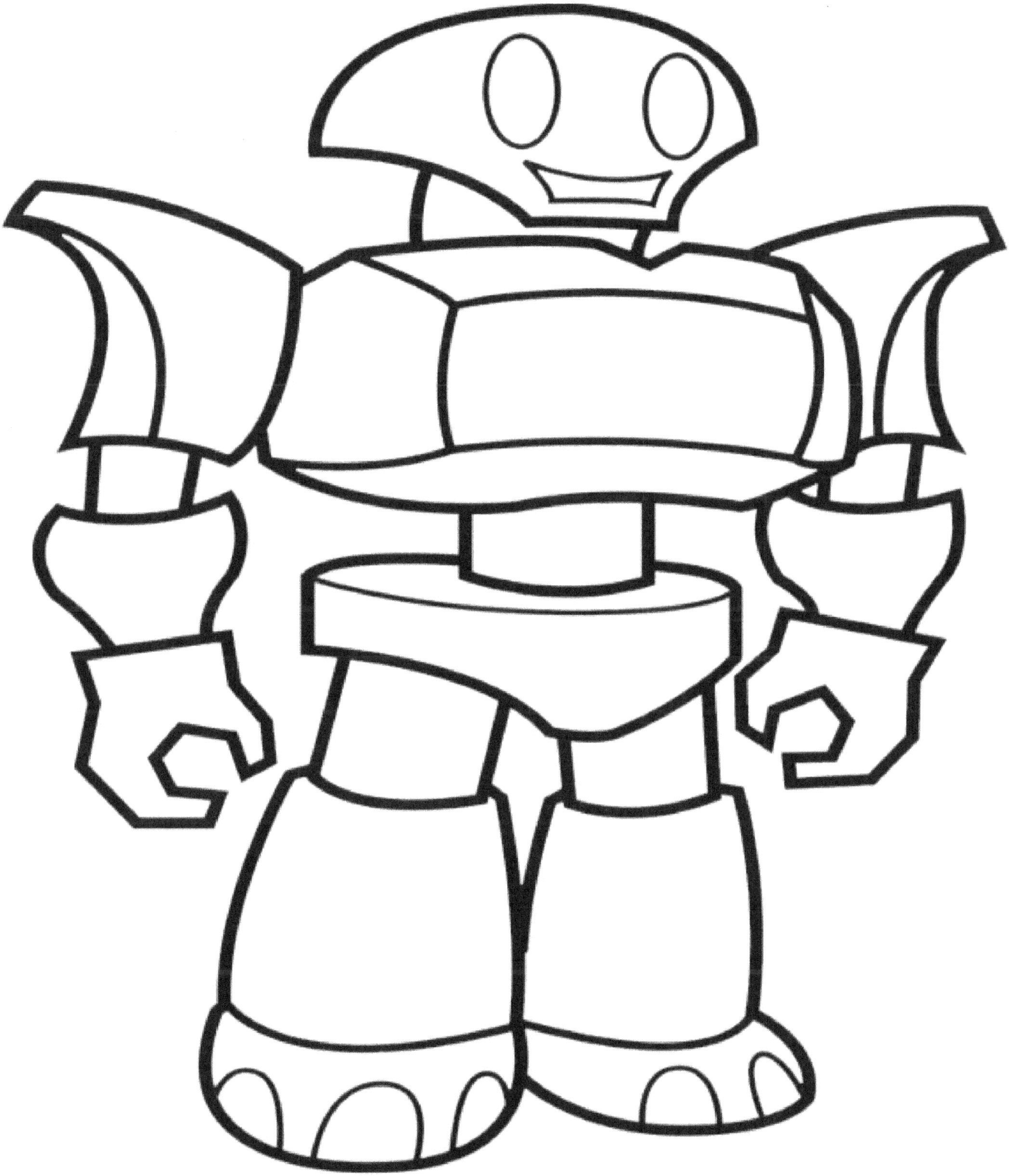

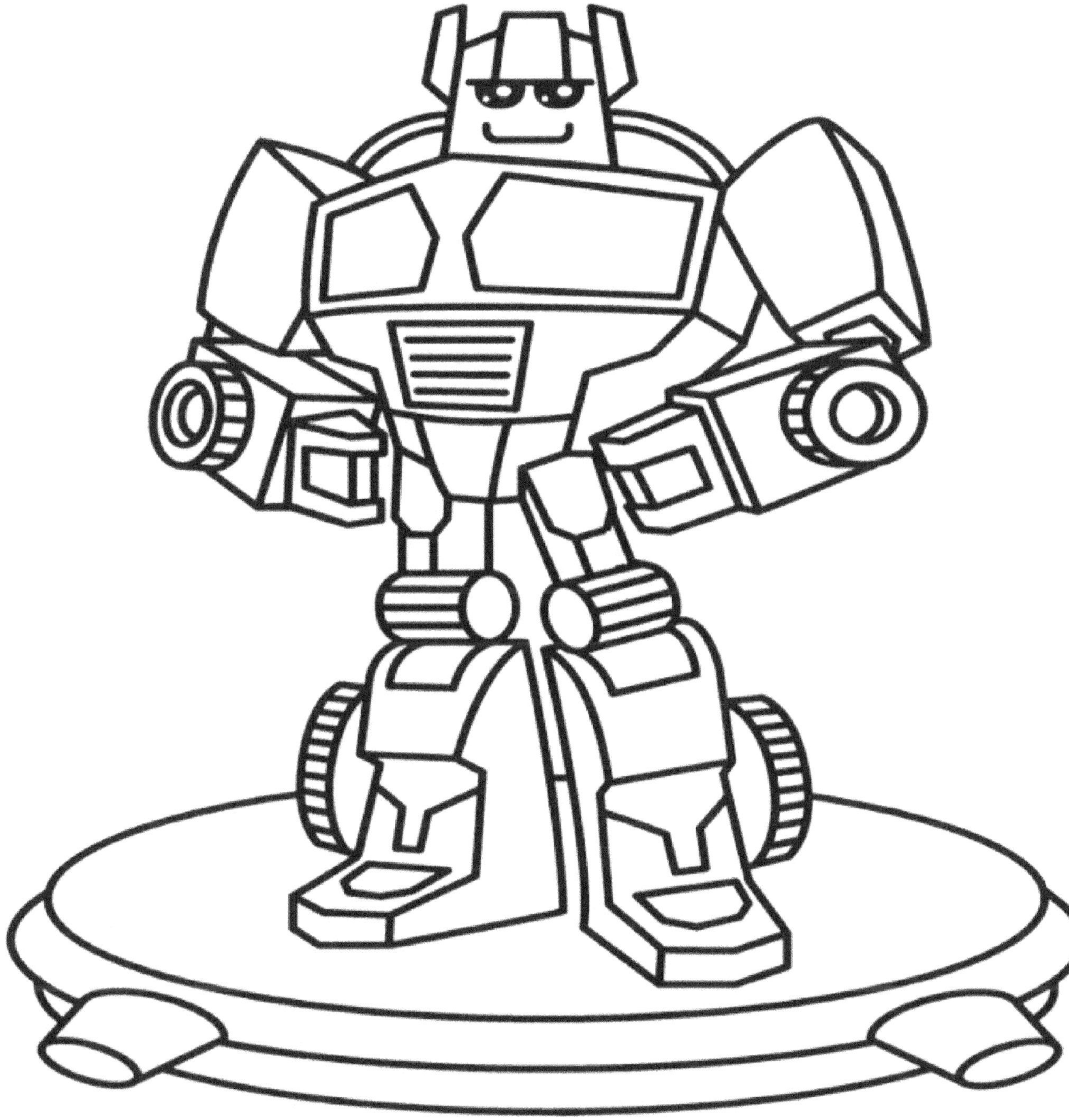

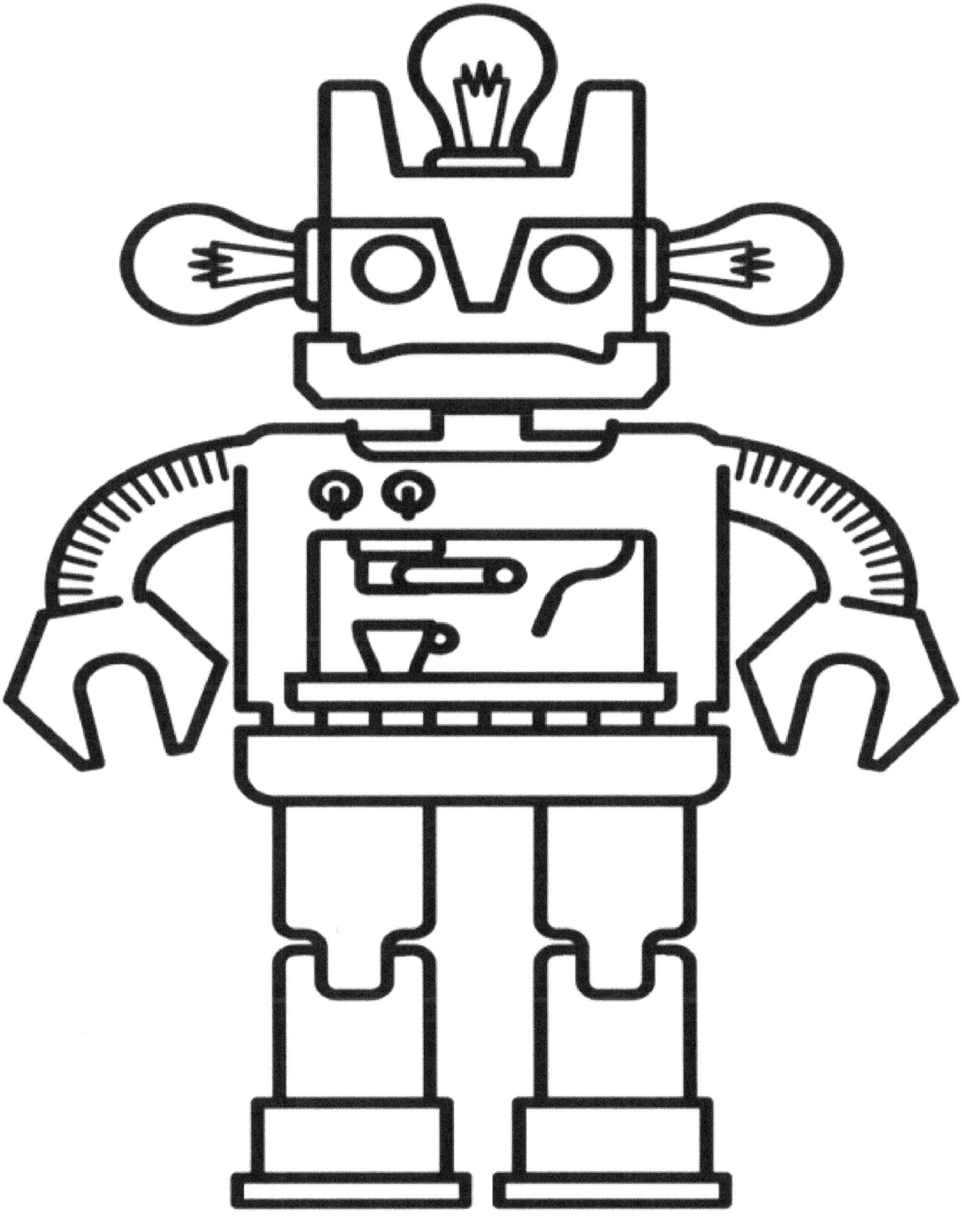

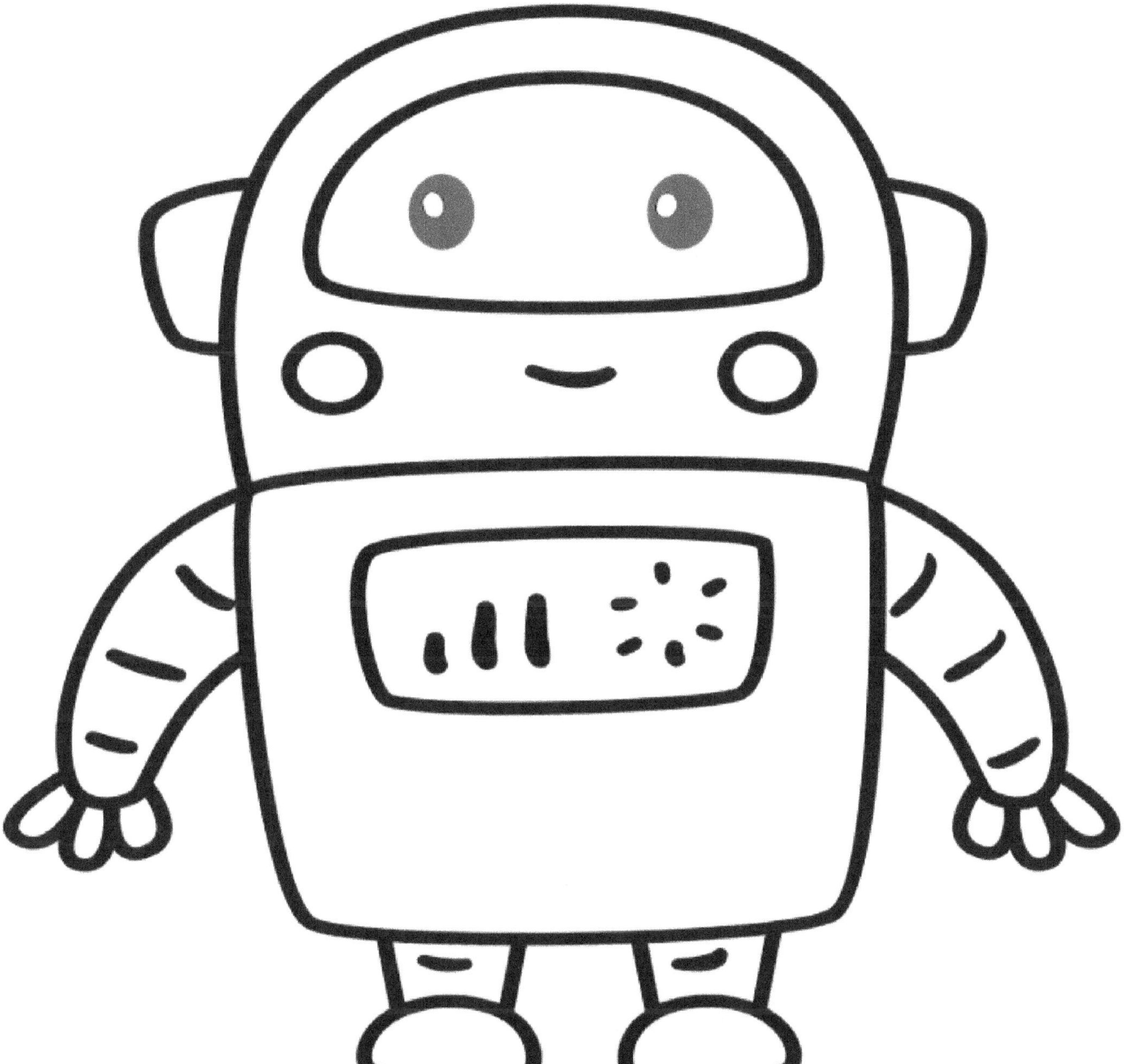

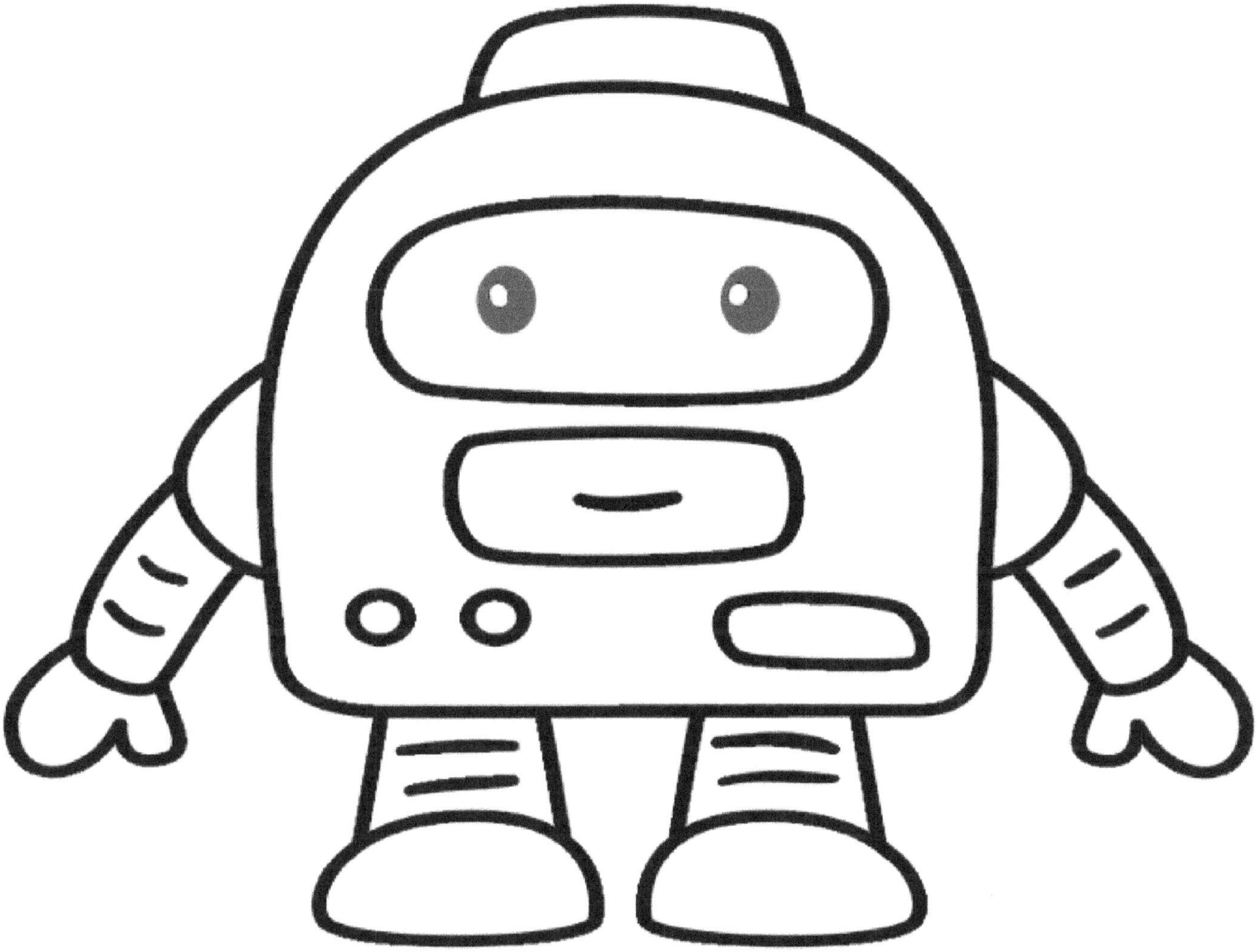

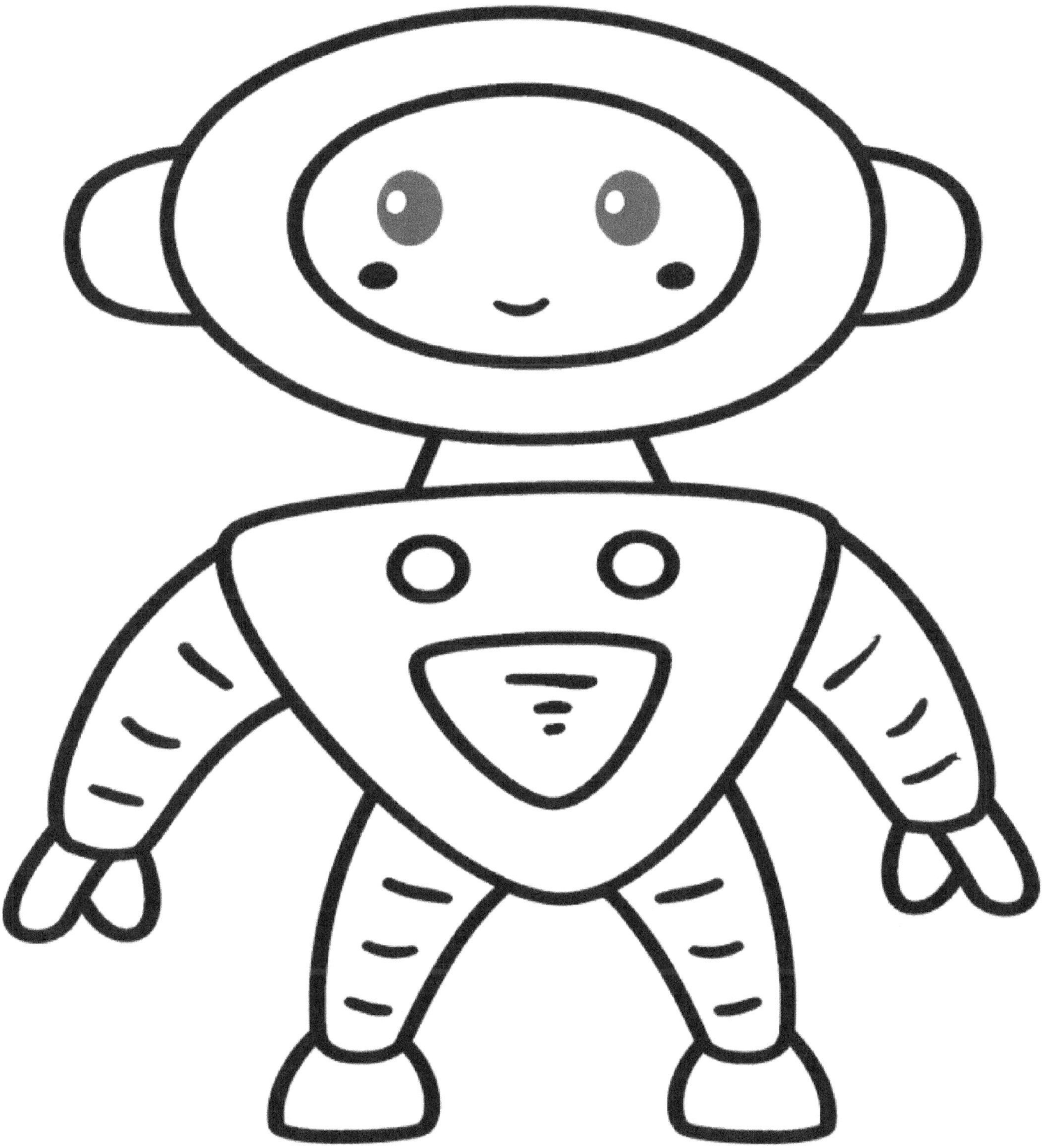

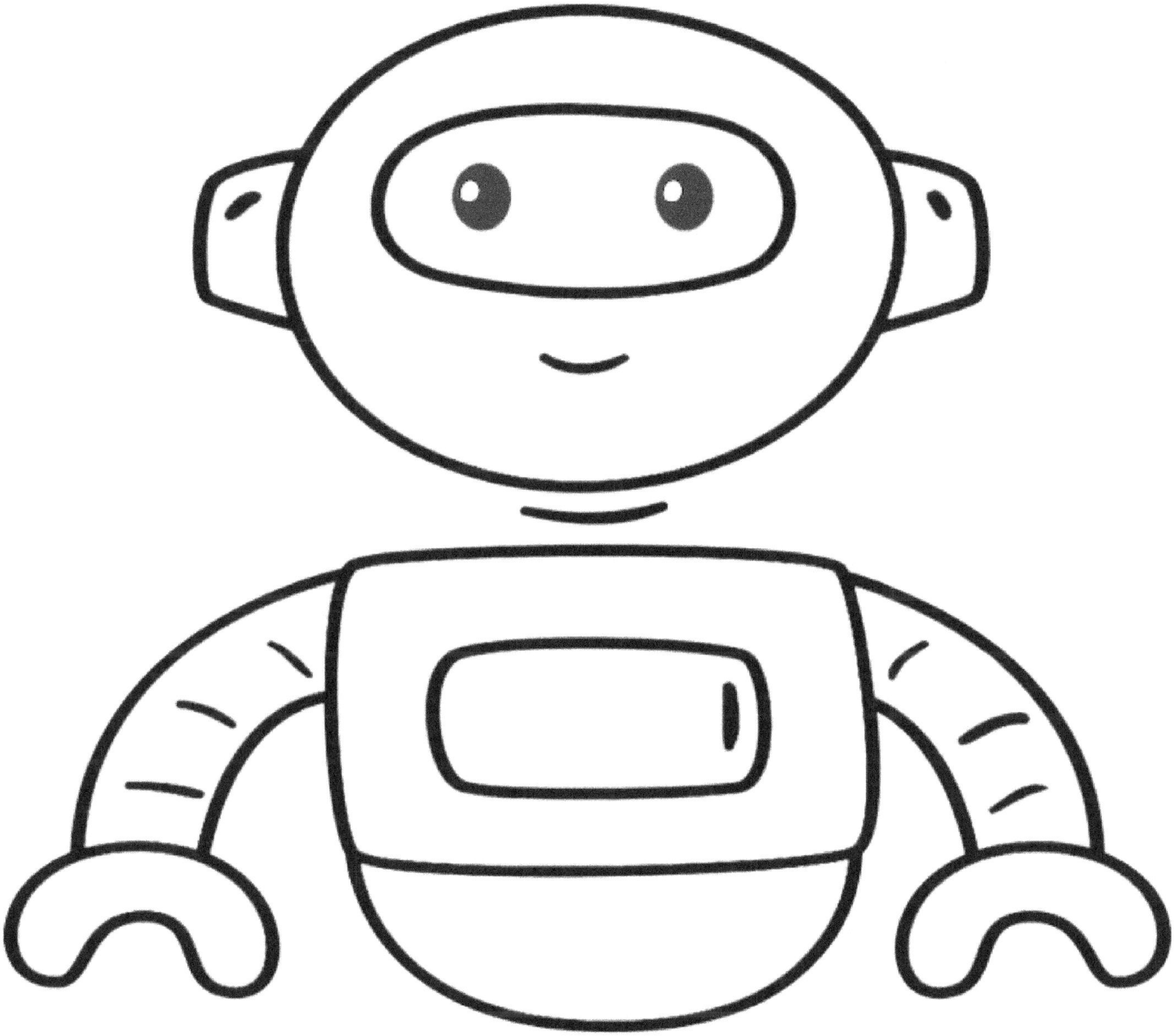

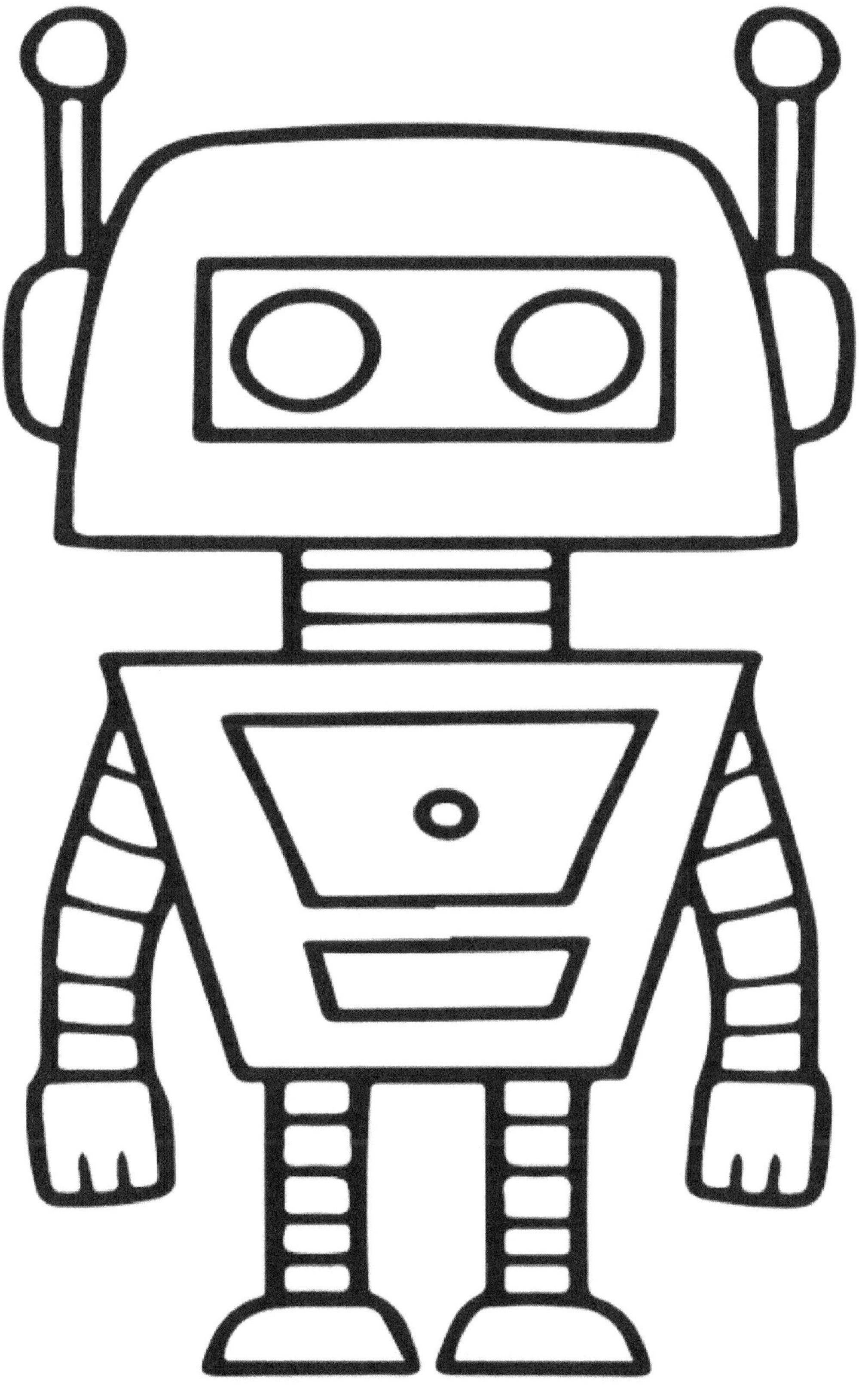

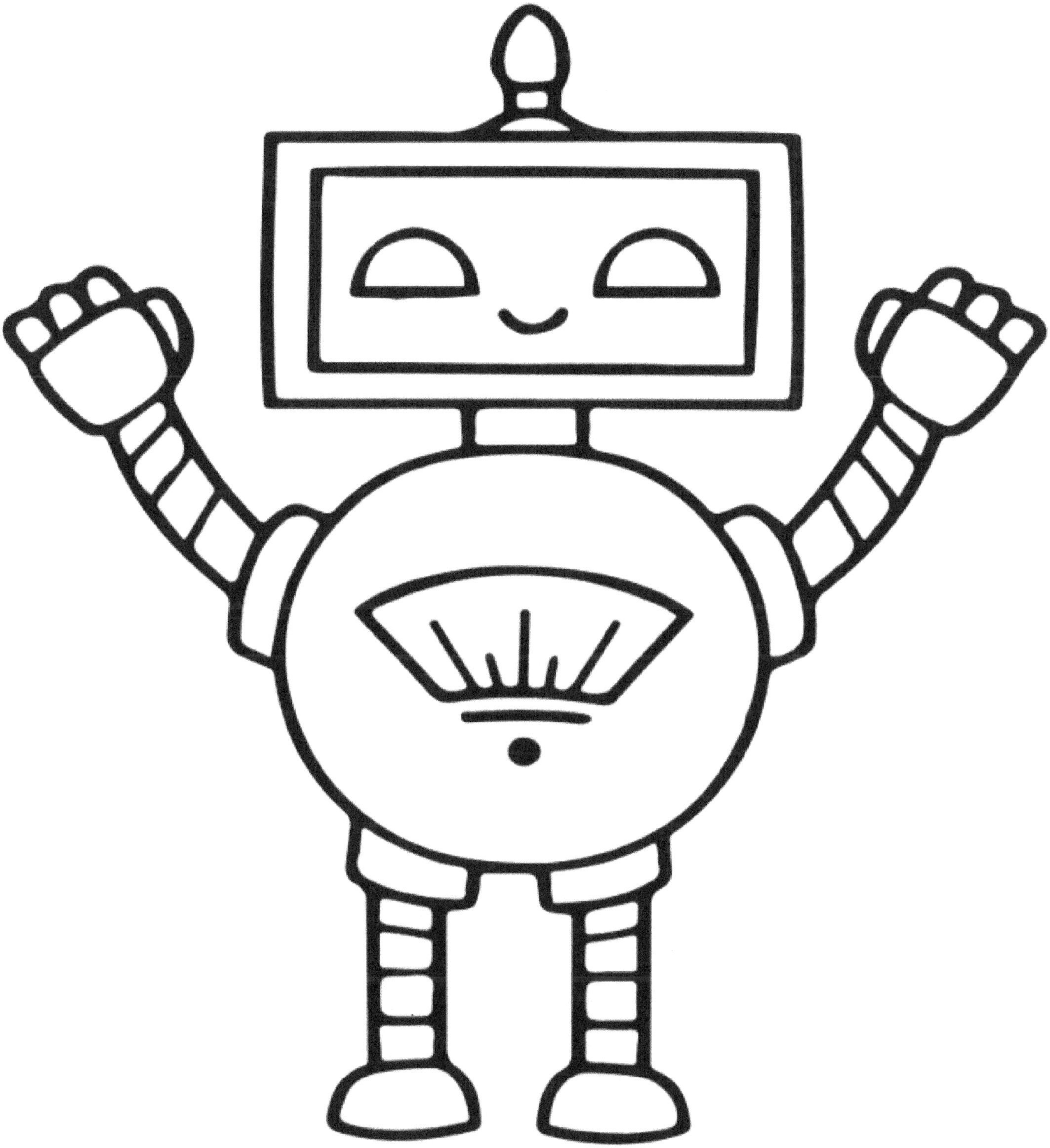

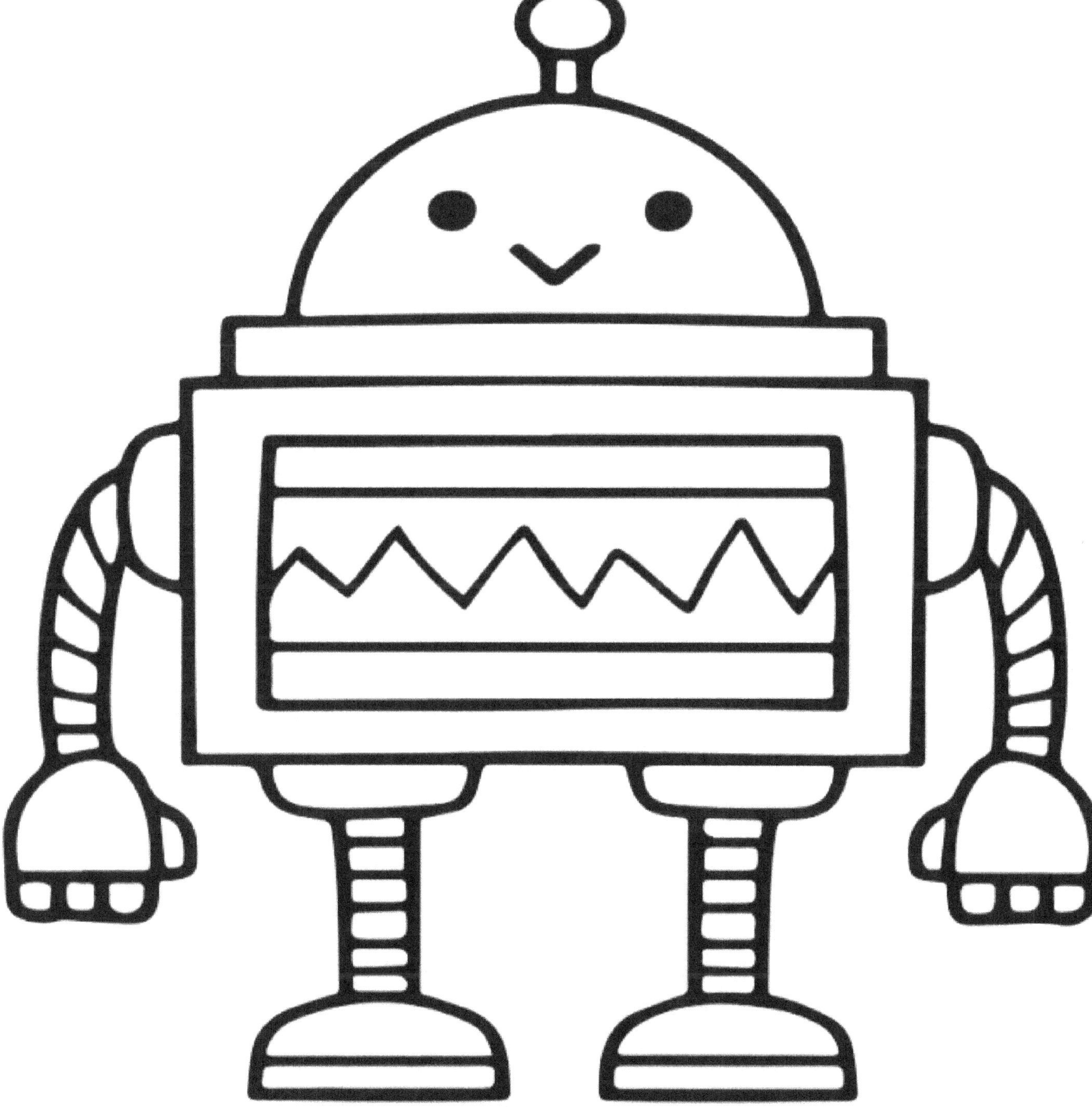

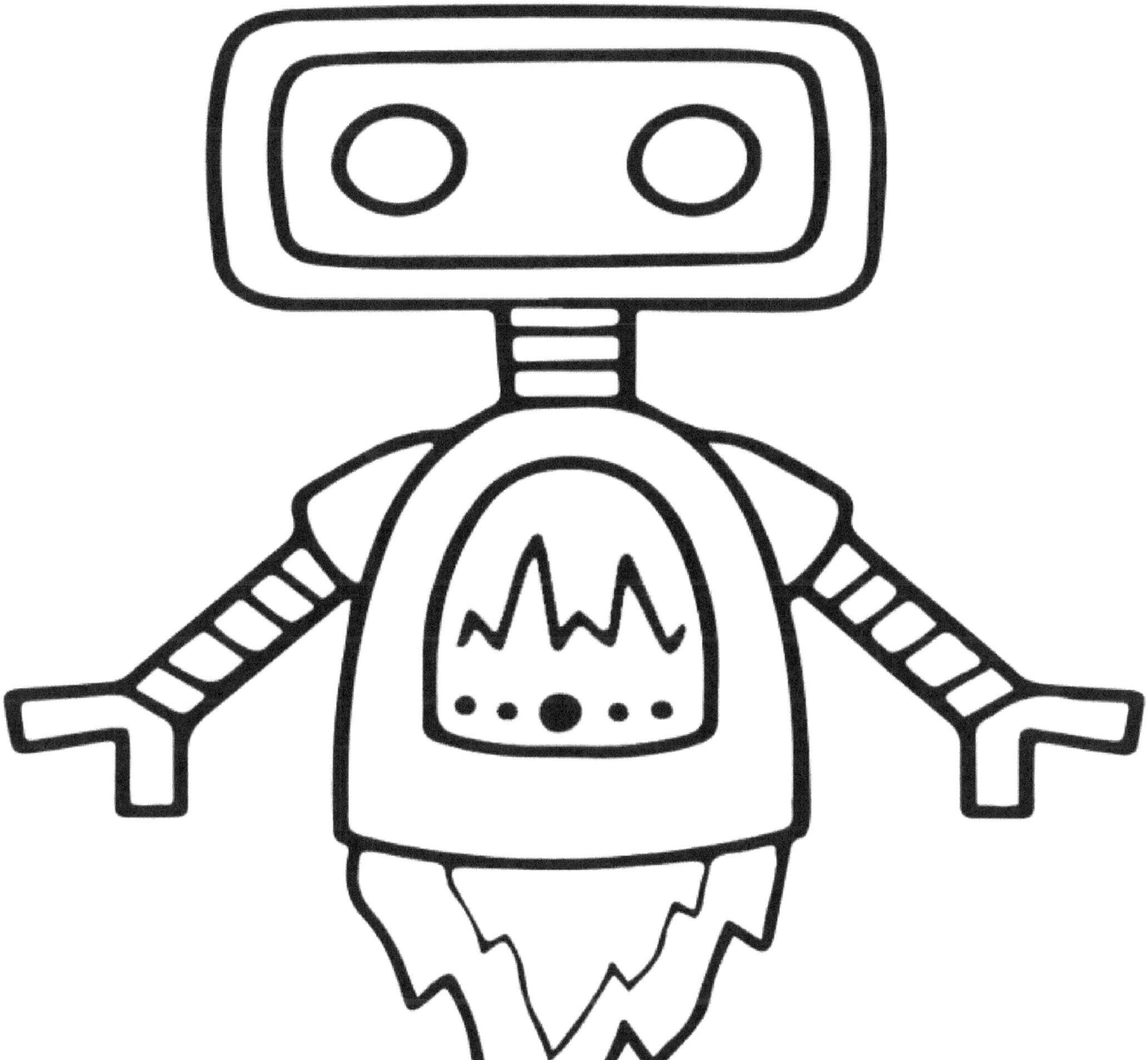

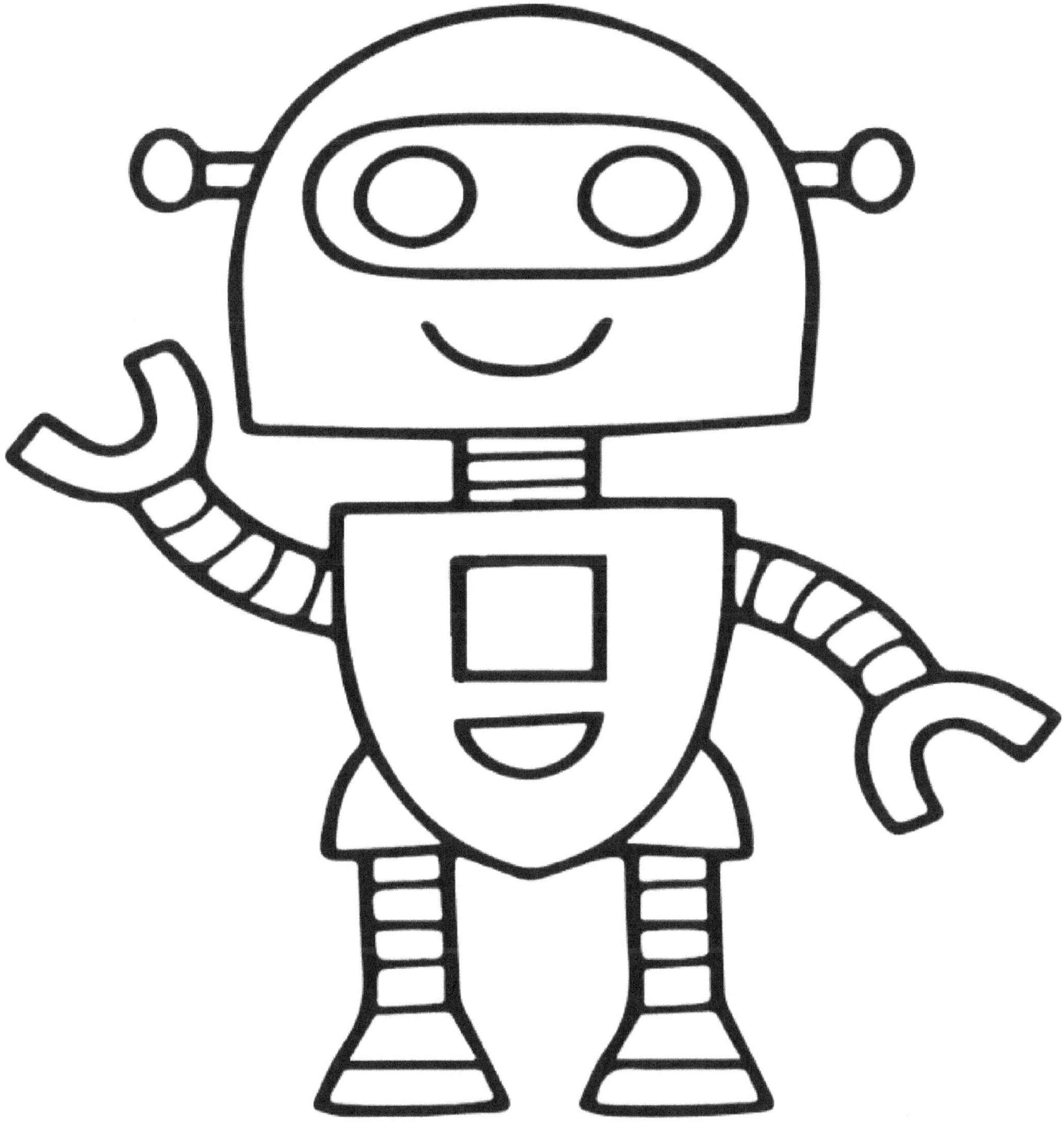

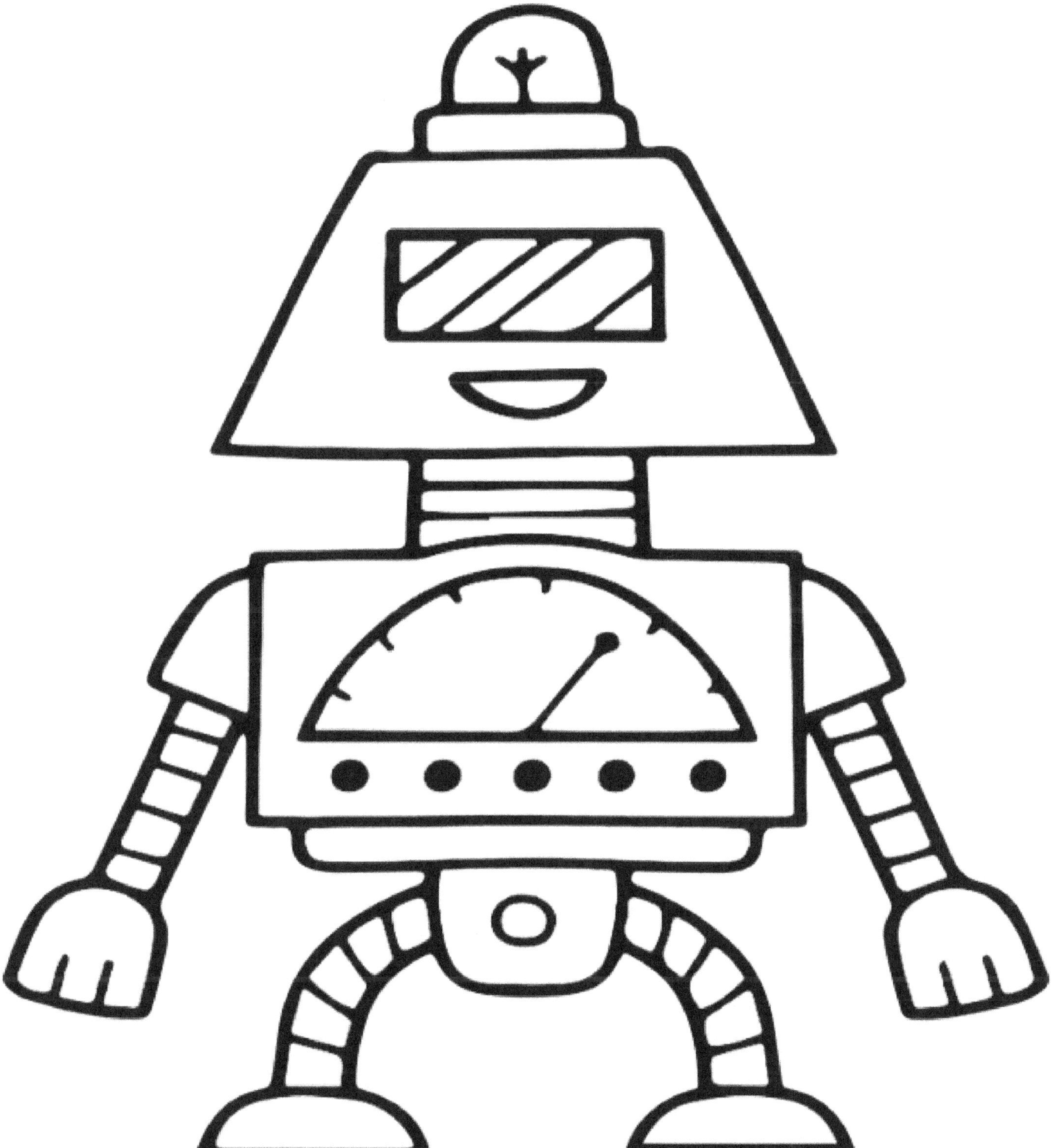

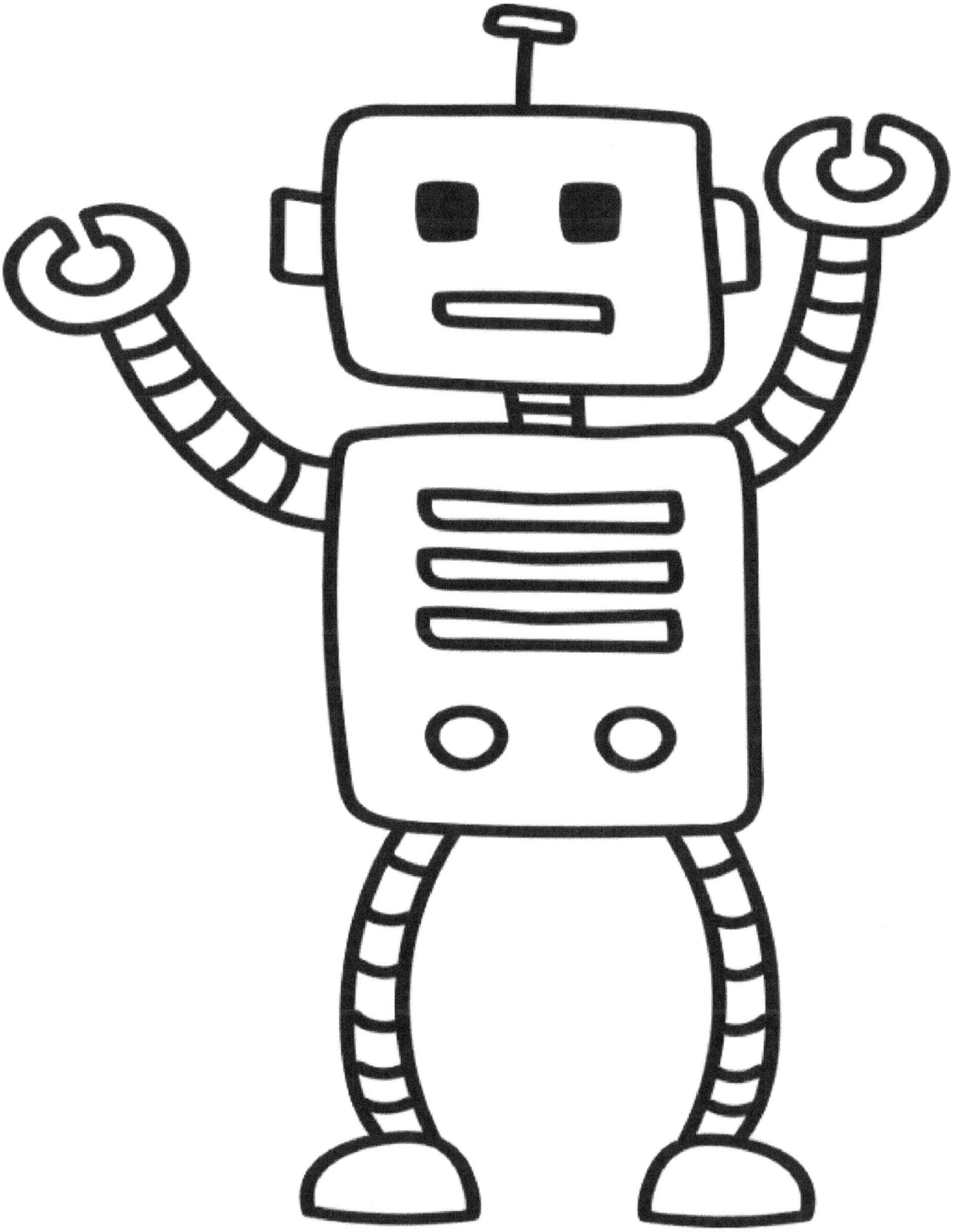

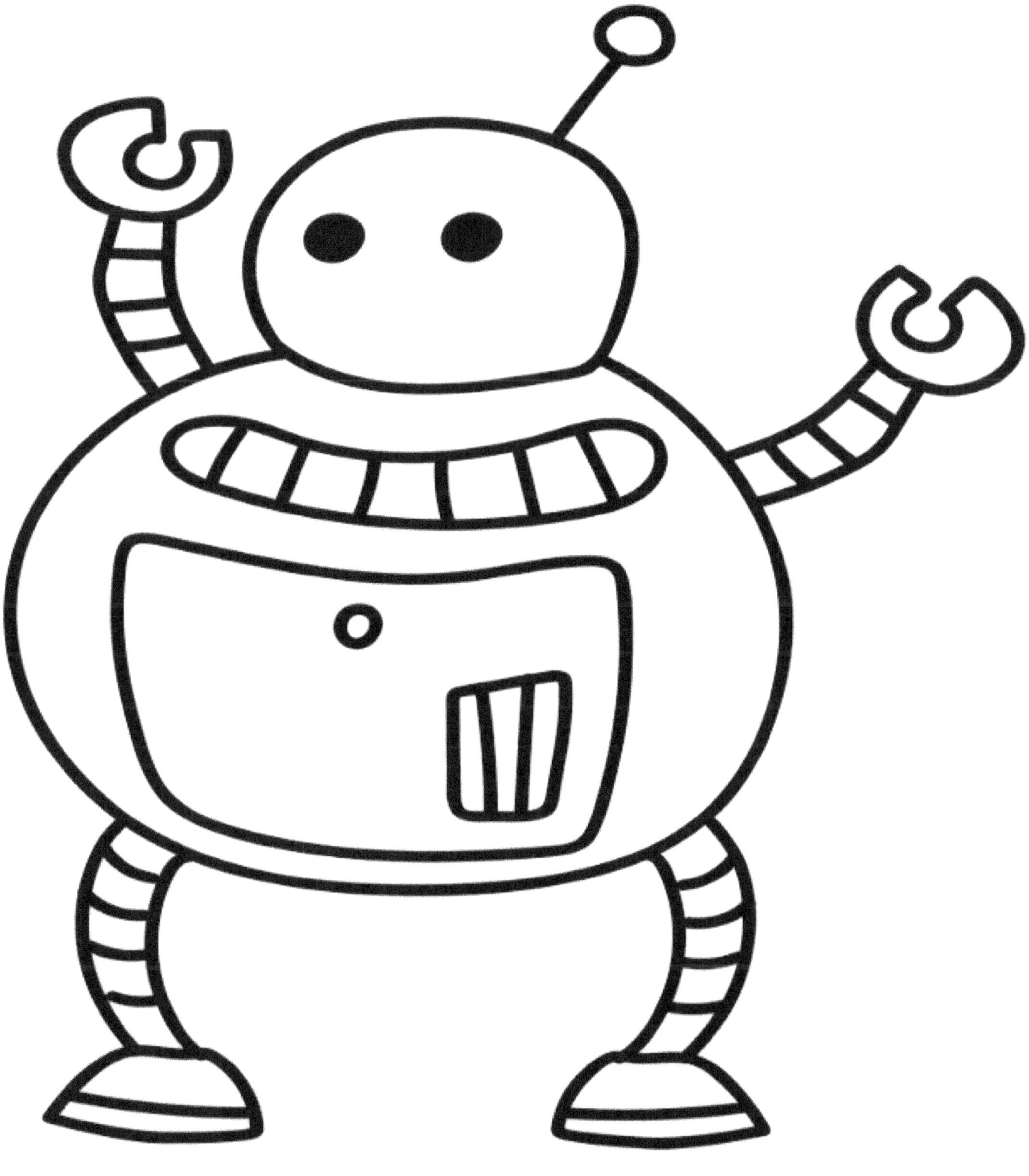

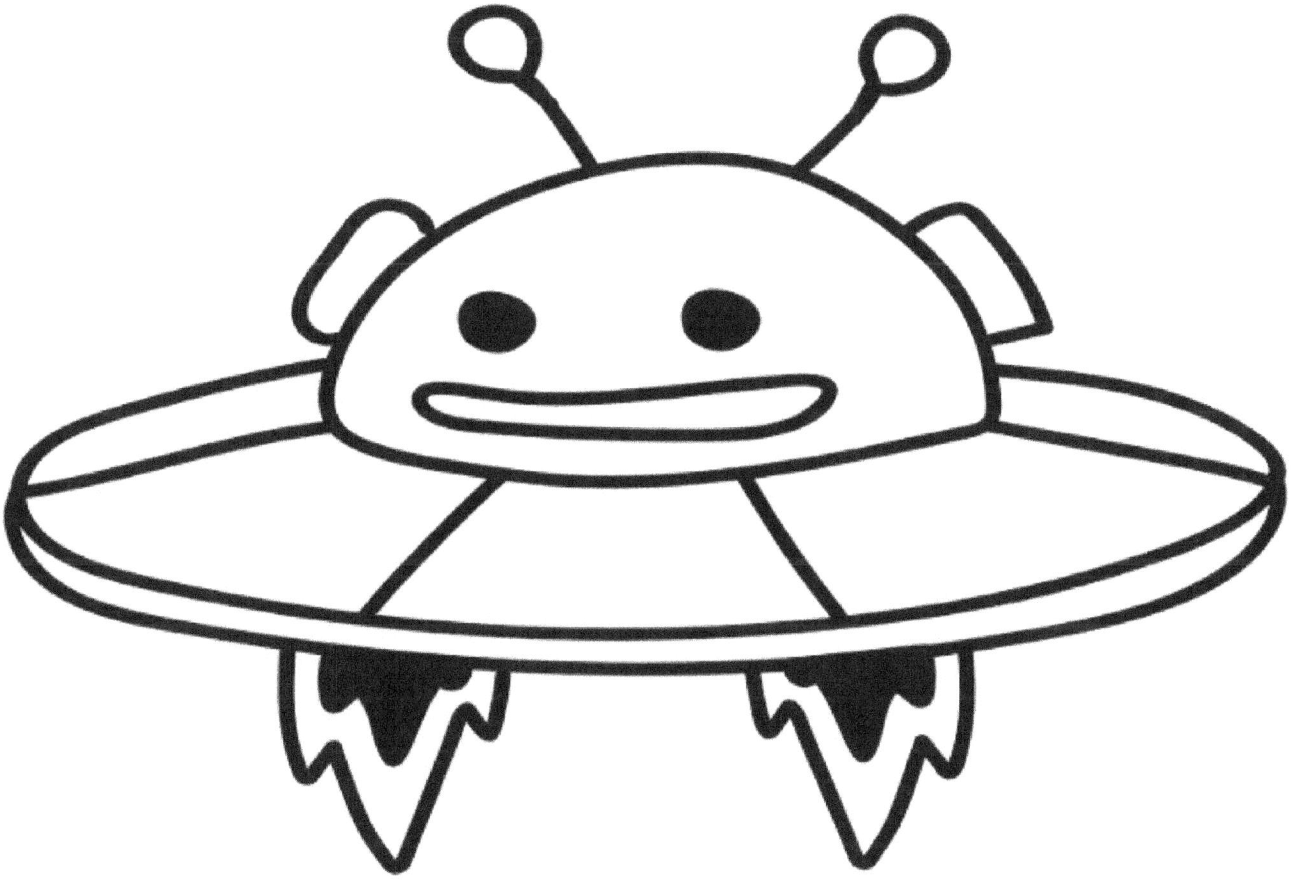

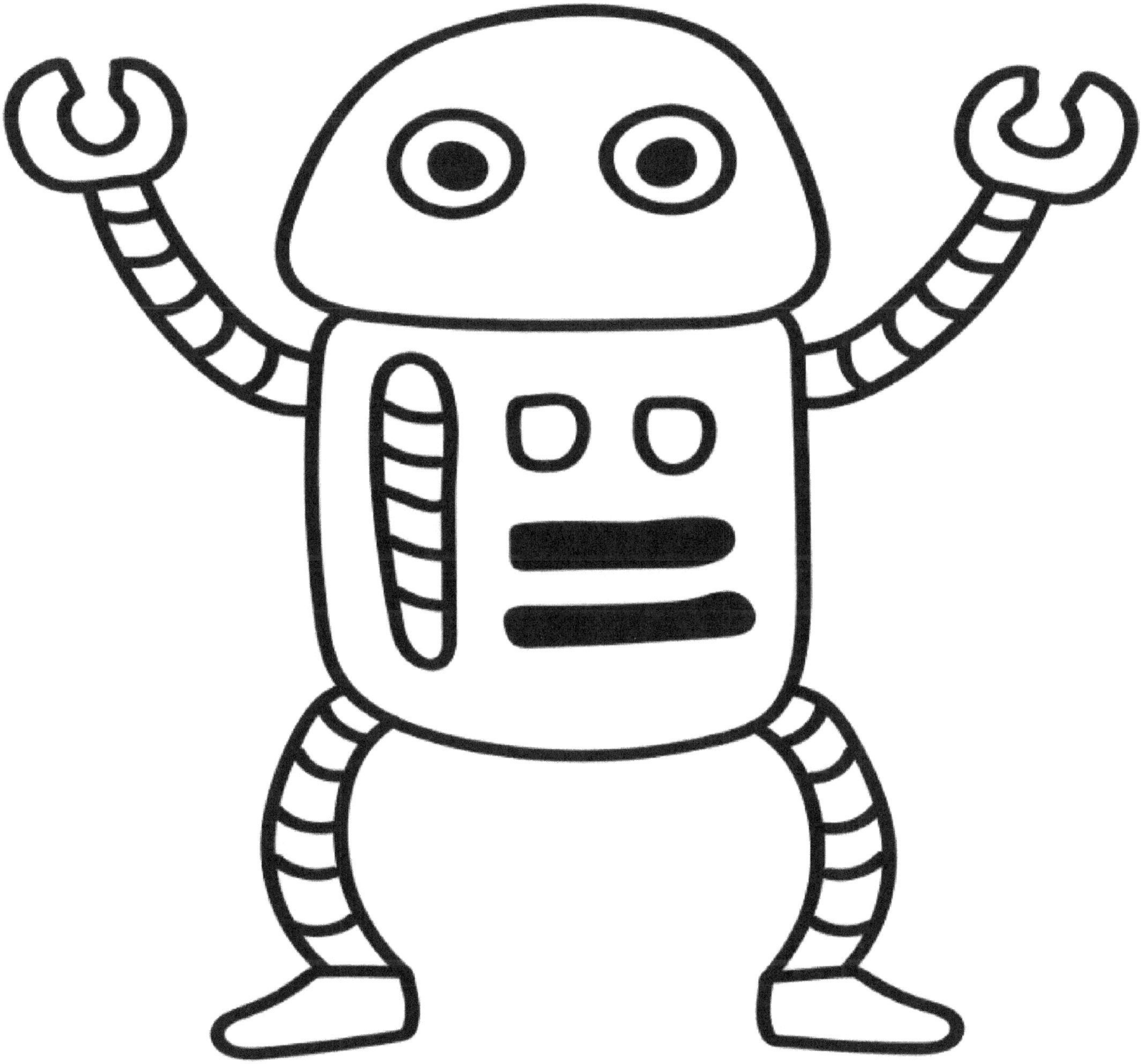

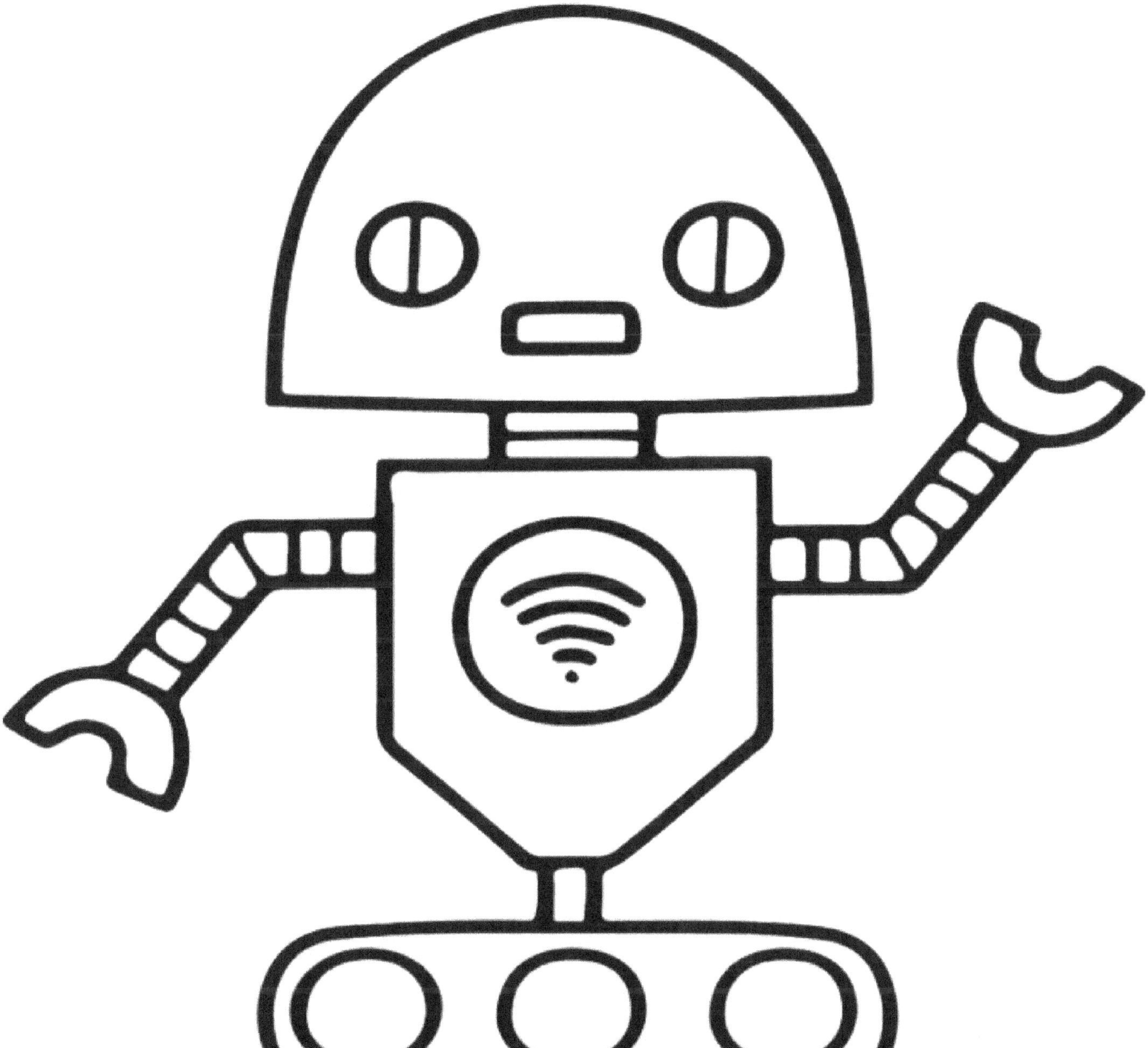

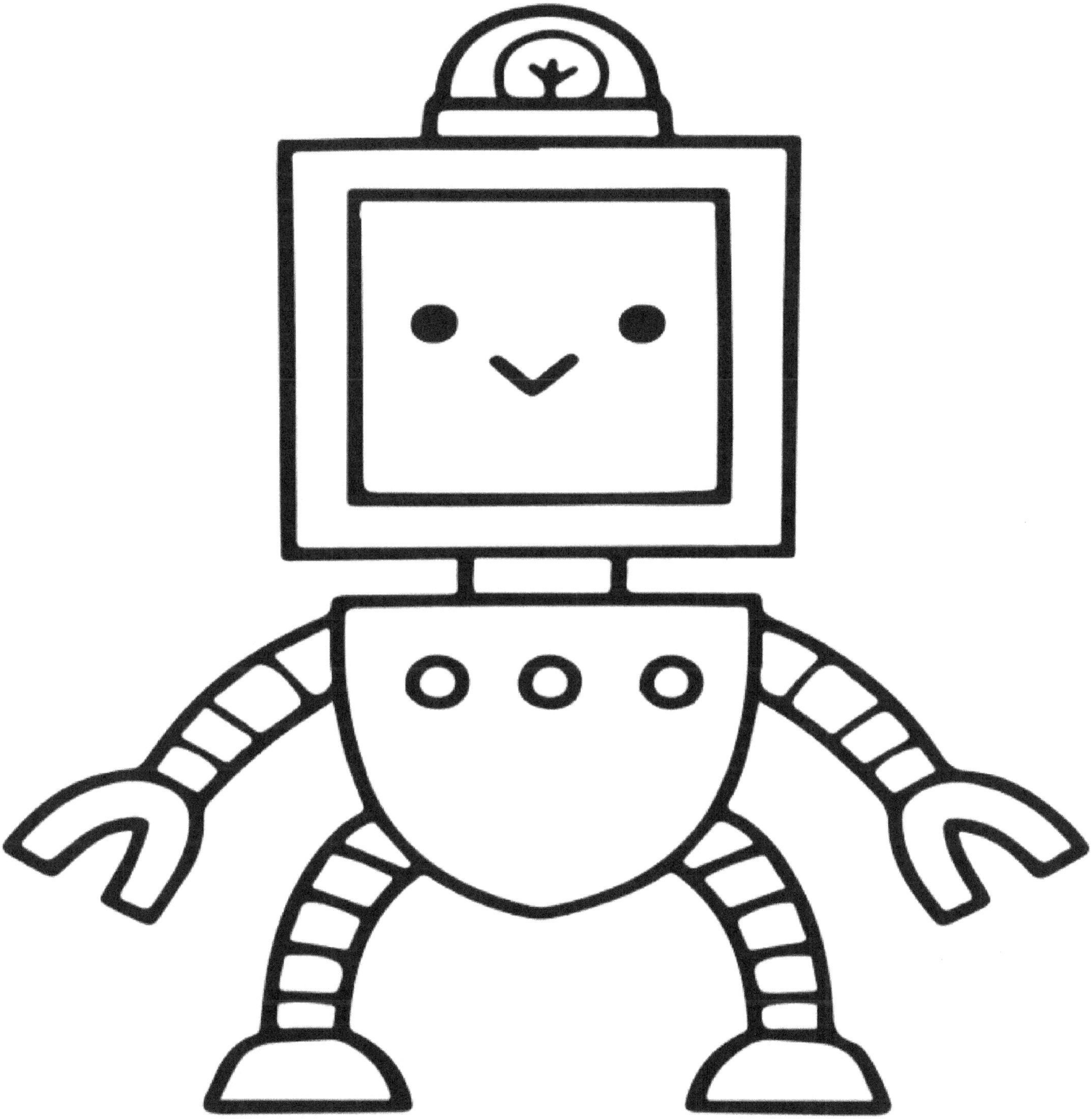

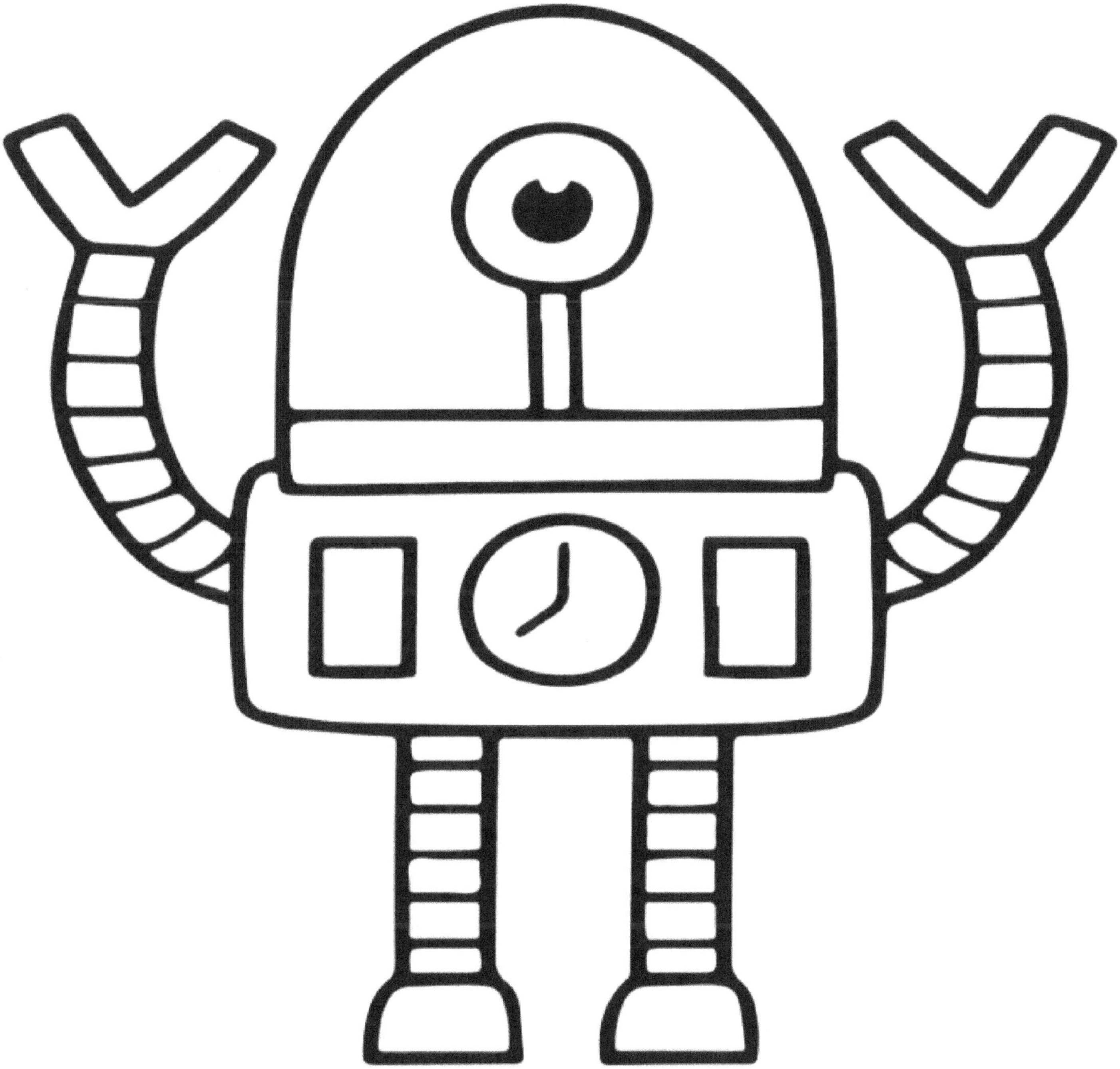

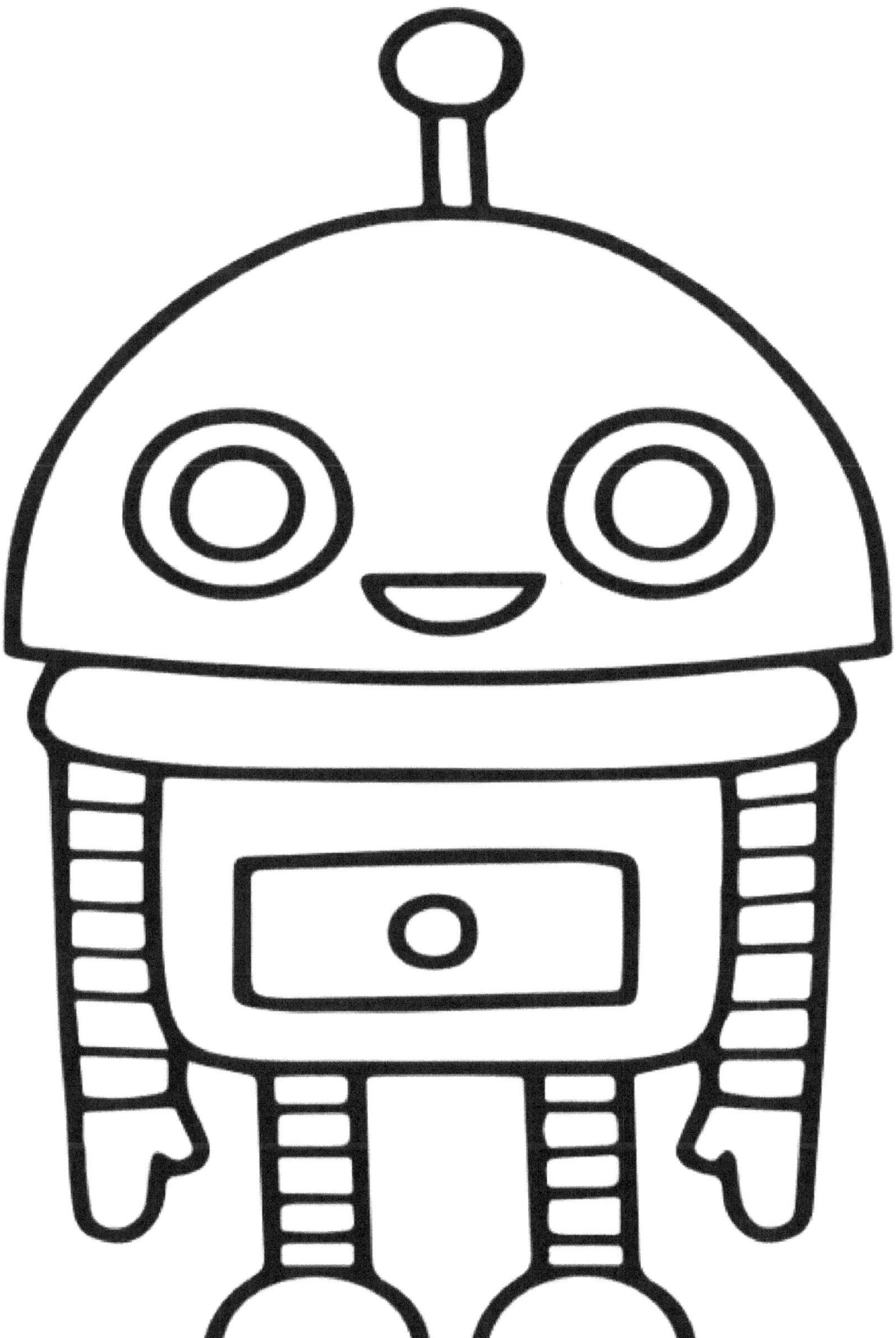

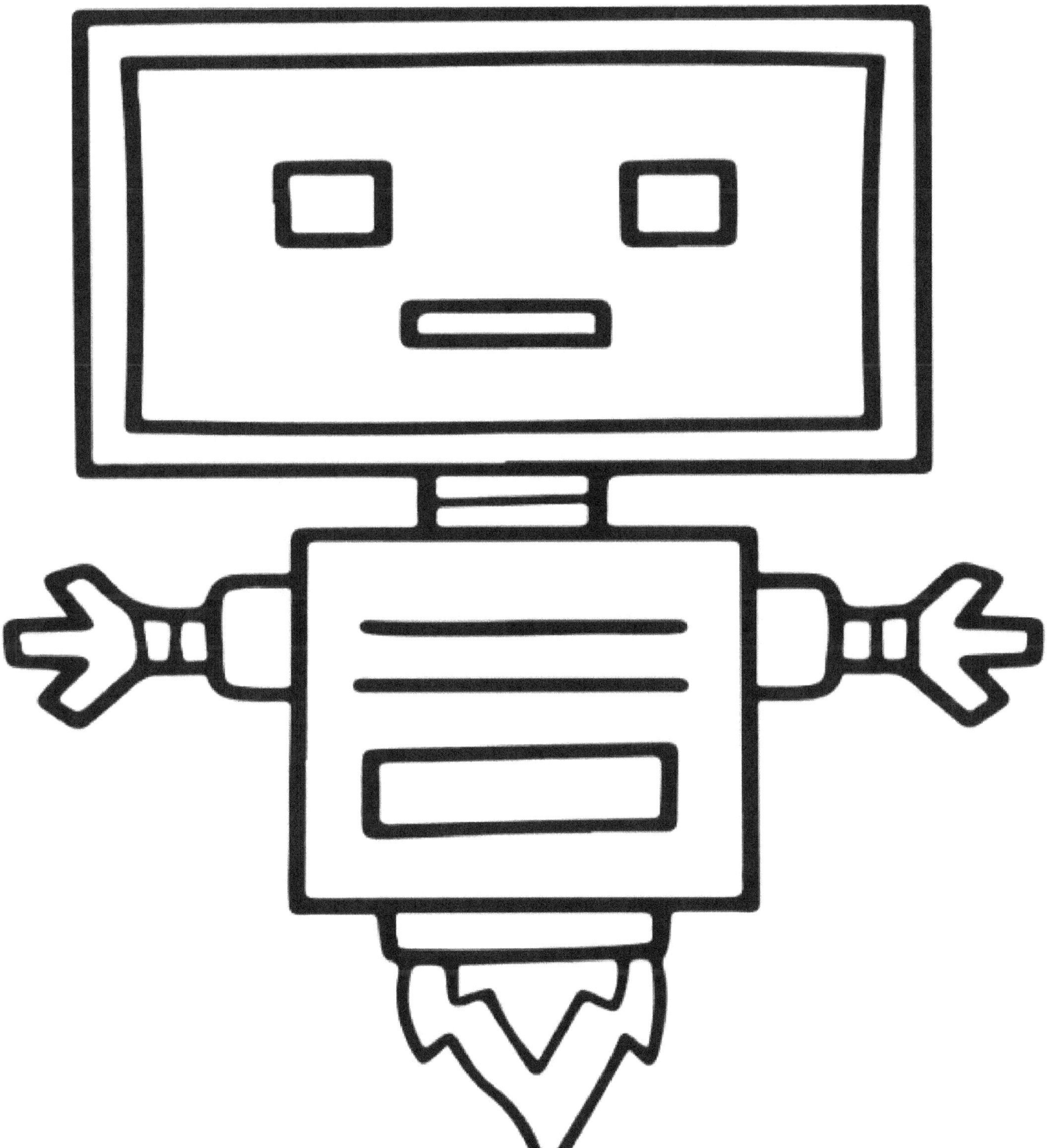

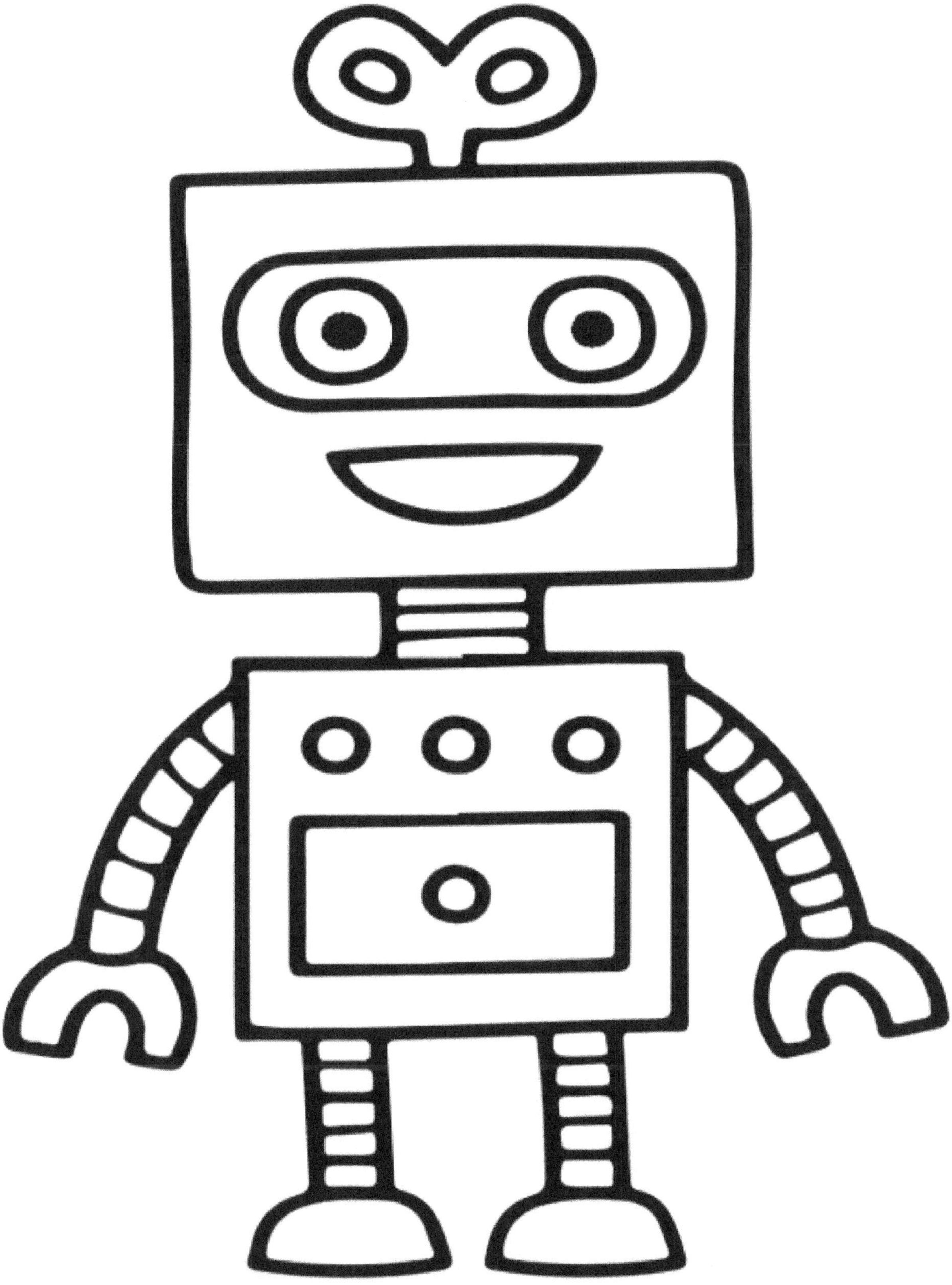

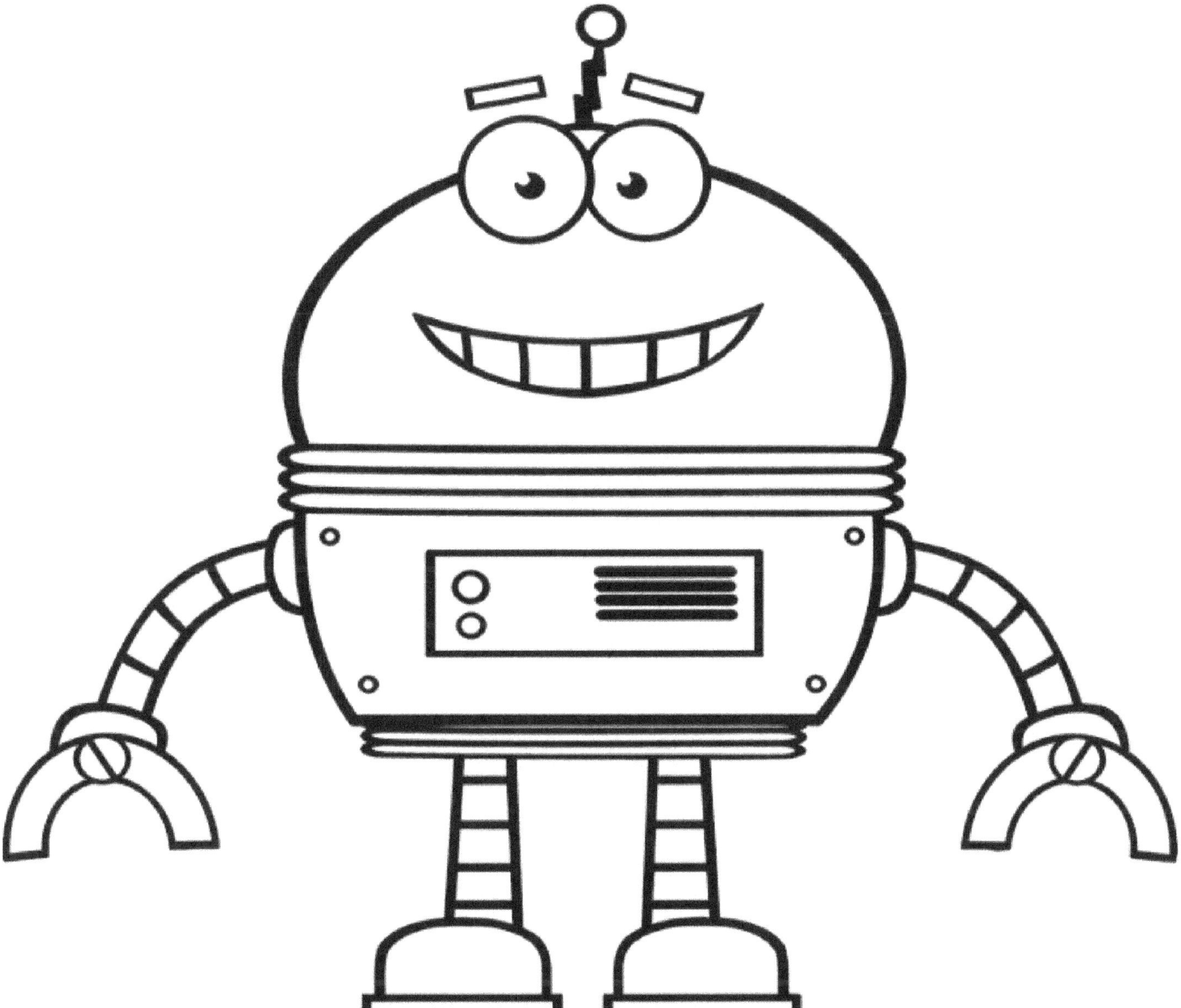

www.ingramcontent.com/pod-product-compliance
Lightning Source LLC
Chambersburg PA
CBHW081536220526
45467CB00010B/3221